Closing the Education Achievement Gap

AEI EVALUATIVE STUDIES
Marvin H. Kosters
Series Editor

Closing the Education Achievement Gap

Is Title I Working?

Marvin H. Kosters
and
Brent D. Mast

The AEI Press

Publisher for the American Enterprise Institute

WASHINGTON, D.C.

2003

Available in the United States from the AEI Press, c/o Client Distribution Services, 193 Edwards Drive, Jackson, TN 38301. To order, call toll free: 1-800-343-4499. Distributed outside the United States by arrangement with Eurospan, 3 Henrietta Street, London WC2E 8LU, England.

Library of Congress Cataloging-in-Publication Data
Kosters, Marvin H.
    Closing the education achievement gap : is Title I working? / Marvin H. Kosters and Brent D. Mast.
        p. cm.-- (AEI evaluative studies)
    Includes bibliographical references and index.
    ISBN 0-8447-7165-1 (pbk.)
    1. Children with social disabilities—Education—United States. 2. Academic achievement—United States. 3. Federal aid to education—United States. 4. United States.
Elementary and Secondary Education Act of 1965. I. Mast, Brent D. II. Title.

    LC4091.K67 2003
    379.2'6'0973—dc21

                                                    2003045163

1 3 5 7 9 10 8 6 4 2

Printed in the United States of America

Contents

FIGURES

Foreword

The AEI Evaluative Studies series consists of detailed empirical analyses of government programs and policies in action. Each study documents the history, purposes, operations, and political underpinnings of the program in question; analyzes its costs, consequences, and efficacy in achieving its goals; and presents proposals for reform. The studies are prepared by leading academic students of individual policy fields and are reviewed by scholars, agency officials, and program proponents and critics before publication.

The growth of public policy research in recent decades has been accompanied by a burgeoning of research and writing on proposed policies and those in the initial stages of implementation. Careful evaluation of the large base of existing programs and policies—many of them politically entrenched and no longer at the forefront of policy debate—has suffered from relative neglect. Within the government, program evaluation is typically limited to scrutiny of annual spending levels and of the number and composition of constituents who are served. Insufficient attention is devoted to fundamental questions: whether a program's social or economic goals are being accomplished, whether the goals are worthy and important, and whether they might be better achieved through alternative approaches.

The AEI series aims to redress that imbalance. By examining government programs in action, it aims to direct more academic, political, and public attention to whether we are getting our money's worth from well-established programs and whether current "policy reform" agendas are indeed focused on issues with the greatest potential for improved public welfare.

CHRISTOPHER DEMUTH
President
American Enterprise Institute
for Public Policy Research

Acknowledgments

We are indebted to many who helped up carry out this research. Arnold Goldstein, Steve Gorman, Alfred Rogers, William Sonnenberg, and Stephanie Stullick were helpful in providing data, technical assistance, and advice. The study was improved greatly by comments from Nabeel Alsalam, Douglas Besharov, Thomas Downes, Sheila Murray, Susan Neuman, Maris Vinovskis, and other participants in a workshop at the American Enterprise Institute.

The analysis also benefited from comments by Mark Berends, Chester Finn, Richard Fry, Nora Gordon, Eric Hanushek, Kevin Hassett, D. Gale Johnson, John Lott, and Sam Peltzman. Valuable research assistance was provided by Rassa Ahmadi, Elizabeth Bax, Jimin Chung, Katherine Moran, Emily Neubig, Elizabeth Rha, Ashley Schumaker, and Kelly Smith, who were interns at AEI. We thank Edward Cowan and Ann Petty for their suggestions in editing the manuscript. We are responsible for any errors that remain.

1

Introduction

On April 11, 1965, President Lyndon Johnson signed into law the Elementary and Secondary Education Act. The act's major provision, generally known as Title I, authorized more than a billion dollars of federal money a year to improve the education of children from low-income families. The law declared that U.S. policy was "to provide financial assistance . . . to local educational agencies serving areas with concentrations of children from low-income families to expand and improve their educational programs by various means . . . which contribute to meeting the special educational needs of educationally deprived children."[1] The two key elements were the distribution of funds and the designation of recipients of the services financed by the act.

The legislation provided for the first time federal financial support to be distributed broadly to elementary and secondary schools across the country. Title I was targeted toward students in schools with disproportionate concentrations of children from low-income families. Those federal funds financed supplementary resources to bring up the achievement levels of Title I children so they would compare more favorably with children from other schools. The fact that aid was aimed toward lower-achieving children and the inclusion of private schools in the program overcame traditional objections to federal funding of what had been primarily the responsibility of state and local governments (Jennings 2000).

Thirty-eight years and more than $200 billion later, what has the program accomplished? Has the program achieved its goals? Does the evidence point to worthwhile progress toward important educational goals? More generally, does the evidence suggest that the federal funds were well spent? Have we been getting our money's worth? This study

1

addresses those questions by describing Title I policies and their implementation, by reviewing other evaluations of the program's performance,
and by developing a new analysis of the effects on students' educational
achievement of participation in Title I in recent years.

Educational achievement and economic status have been recognized as closely linked, both because areas with high-income families
can provide more resources for schools and because achievement has
generally been lower in schools with many children from low-income
families. The rationale for Title I was that making more resources available to children in high-poverty schools could boost their achievement.
Because schools with high concentrations of children from poor families
tend to have disproportionate shares of minority children, a program
that succeeded in improving achievement in high-poverty schools would
also help reduce the achievement gap for minority children.

Policies that could successfully raise educational achievement of
poor and minority children, and thus reduce measured gaps in achievement, would make an extraordinarily valuable contribution to society.
Reducing or eliminating systematic gaps in achievement by breaking into
a cycle of low expectations and achievement could contribute to improving the economic status of those affected and reducing racial disparities in
education and income. That is a constructive and important objective. The
goal of Title I notwithstanding, the main issues are whether the program
actually improves educational achievement and whether any such
improvement is sufficient to make Title I worthwhile in relation to its costs.

Measures of gaps in achievement illustrate the dimensions of
the problem and indicate in broad terms whether progress is being
achieved. Analyses of the effects of Title I on achievement described and
presented later in this book provide more direct evidence of the extent
to which the program has contributed to reducing gaps in achievement.

Achievement Gaps

The achievement gaps that motivated the enactment of Title I remain sizable.
The levels of achievement of children in low-poverty and high-poverty
schools illustrate how far children from low-income schools fall behind

other children.[2] The Department of Education scaled the achievement levels measured by National Assessment of Educational Progress (NAEP) tests to represent four levels of achievement: below basic, basic, proficient, and advanced. Figures 1-1 and 1-2, respectively, display the proportions of fourth-grade children who score well enough to reach those different levels of achievement in reading (1998) and math (1996).[3] It is apparent from those figures that children from high-poverty schools are heavily over-represented in the below-basic category. For high-poverty schools, a large majority of students fail to achieve skills even at the basic level, while only about one-fifth of the children from low-poverty schools score as poorly. A smaller percentage of children from high-poverty schools than low-poverty schools achieve basic skill levels. Few children from high-poverty schools achieve proficient and advanced levels. The data clearly show that Title I and other compensatory education programs have failed to bring up the achievement of children from high-poverty schools to levels comparing favorably with schools where families are better off.

In addition, nothing indicates that gaps in achievement between children from low- and high-poverty schools have been reduced in recent years. Figures 1-3 and 1-4, respectively, show measures of disparities in achievement for fourth-grade children in reading and math.[4] The figures show trends from 1986 (math) and 1988 (reading) to 1999 in the gaps between average scores for all students in the sample and average scores for children from low- and high-proverty schools.[5] The figures suggest that achievement gaps for children from schools with different levels of family income have widened somewhat since the 1980s. By 1999 the gap for reading scores was about a full standard deviation, and the gap for math scores, about eight-tenths of a standard deviation. Although the size of the gap is larger for reading than for math, the trends are not very different. Stagnation or possible deterioration took place during a period with moderate growth in funding and substantial reform of the implementation of Title I programs.

Concomitant patterns of differences in performance between racial groups underscore the significance of concerns about the performance of schools with children from different income strata. Figures 1-5 and 1-6 display achievement categories for black and white children in the fourth

Figure 1-1 Fourth-Grade Reading Skills by School Poverty Level, 1998

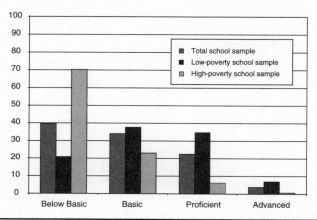

NOTE: *High-poverty schools* are defined as those with more than 75 percent of students eligible for subsidized lunches. *Low-poverty schools* are those with no more than 25 percent of students eligible.

SOURCE: Authors' calculations based on state NAEP restricted data for fourth-grade reading, 1998.

Figure 1-2 Fourth-Grade Math Skills by School Poverty Level, 1996

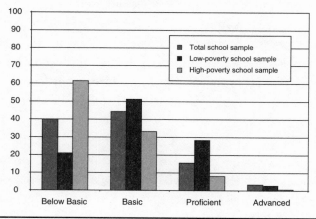

NOTE: *High-poverty schools* are defined as those with more than 75 percent of students eligible for subsidized lunches. *Low-poverty schools* are those with no more than 25 percent of students eligible.

SOURCE: Authors' calculations based on state NAEP restricted data for fourth-grade math, 1996.

Figure 1-3 Test Score Gaps by School Poverty Level for Fourth-Grade NAEP Reading Tests, 1988–1999

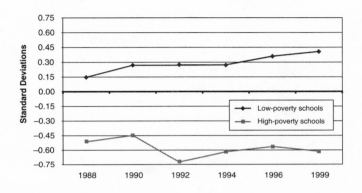

NOTE: Measures of gaps are computed from comparisons with average scores. *High-poverty schools* are defined as those with more than 75 percent of students eligible for subsidized lunches. *Low-poverty schools* are those with no more than 25 percent of students eligible.

SOURCE: DOE, PES 2000a and NCES, 2002.

Figure 1-4 Test Score Gaps by School Poverty Level for Fourth-Grade NAEP Math Tests, 1986–1999

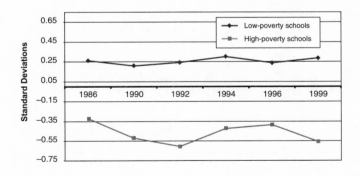

NOTE: Measures of gaps are computed from comparisons with average scores. *High-poverty schools* are defined as those with more than 75 percent of students eligible for subsidized lunches. *Low-poverty schools* are those with no more than 25 percent of students eligible.

SOURCE: DOE, PES 2001a and NCES, 2002.

Figure 1-5 Fourth-Grade Reading Skills by Race, 1998

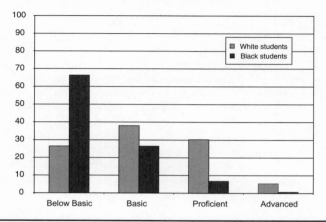

SOURCE: Authors' calculations using state NAEP restricted data for fourth-grade reading, 1998.

Figure 1-6 Fourth-Grade Math Skills by Race, 1996

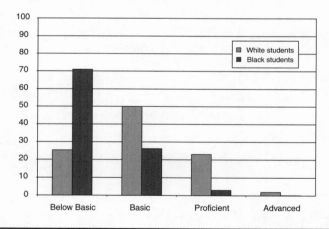

SOURCE: Authors' calculations using state NAEP restricted data for fourth-grade math, 1996.

grade.[6] As with comparisons between low- and high-poverty schools, differences in achievement between white and black children are quite pronounced. The pattern of deficiencies in performance levels achieved by black children resembles that for children from high-poverty schools. Large majorities of black students fail to master skills at the basic level for reading and for math compared with only about a quarter of white students. Only a tiny percentage of black students master skills in proficient and advanced categories. If Title I programs have any impact on programs on the black-white test score gaps, they certainly fall far short of closing the gap.

Figures 1-7 and 1-8 show the trends in gaps in average achievement between black and white children for reading (since 1971) and math skills (since 1978).[7] A promising reduction in the achievement gaps between black and white students occurred during the 1970s and the first part of the 1980s according to reading test score data. Math test scores show similar trends for the shorter period from 1978 to 1986. However, for both reading and math and for both fourth and eighth graders, the achievement gaps between black and white students showed no further sustained reduction after the mid-1980s.[8] The size of achievement gaps for both reading and math for fourth graders stayed within a fairly narrow range from the mid-1980s until the end of the 1990s. Achievement gaps for eighth graders widened after the mid-1980s for both kinds of skills. By the late 1990s gaps in test scores between black and white students were more or less similar in magnitude to those prevalent in the early and mid-1980s.

In addition to temporal variation, the performance of minority and poor students shows substantial geographic variation. Figures 1-9 and 1-10 present black-white gaps in NAEP reading (1998) and math (1996) scores for fourth-grade children in participating states.[9] The black-white gaps for reading scores range from a third of a standard deviation in Maine to more than a standard deviation in Wisconsin, Connecticut, and several other states. For math scores, only Vermont and Wyoming show gaps as small as about half a standard deviation, and North Dakota shows a negligible gap. Minnesota, Wisconsin, and several other states show black-white gaps for math scores that are greater than a standard deviation. The size of the test score gaps by race on average compares roughly, as expected, with those in figures 1-7 and 1-8. However, the size of the gaps varies considerably among states, perhaps in part because racial socioeconomic characteristics vary considerably among states.

Figure 1-7 Black-White Test Score Gaps for NAEP Reading Tests, 1971–1999

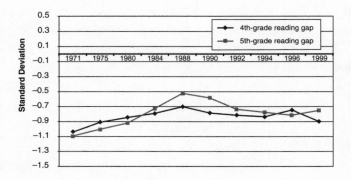

NOTE: Measures of gaps between black and white students are computed from comparisons with average scores for all students. In addition to black and white students, averages for all students include scores for Hispanic, Native American, and Asian students.

SOURCE: DOE, NCES 2000c and 2002.

Figure 1-8 Black-White Test Score Gaps for NAEP Math Tests, 1978–1999

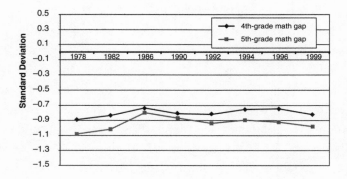

NOTE: Measures of gaps between black and white students are computed from comparisons with average scores for all students. In addition to black and white students, averages for all students include scores for Hispanic, Native American, and Asian students.

SOURCE: DOE, NCES 2000c and 2002.

Figure 1-9 Black-White Test Score Gaps for Fourth-Grade NAEP Reading Tests by State, 1998

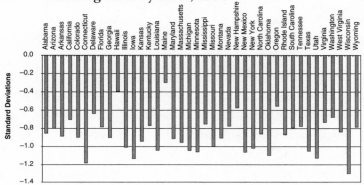

NOTE: Measures of gaps between black and white students are computed from comparisons with average scores for all students. In addition to black and white students, averages for all students include scores for Hispanic, Native American, and Asian students.

SOURCE: Authors' calculations using state NAEP restricted data for fourth-grade reading, 1998

Figure 1-10 Black-White Test Score Gaps for Fourth-Grade NAEP Math Tests by State, 1996

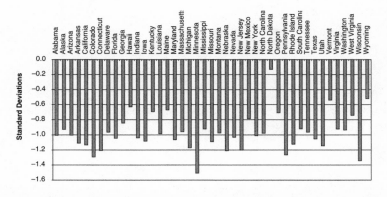

NOTE: Measures of gaps between black and white students are computed from comparisons with average scores for all students. In addition to black and white students, averages for all students include scores for Hispanic, Native American, and Asian students.

SOURCE: Authors' calculations using state NAEP restricted data for fourth-grade math, 1996.

Figures 1-11 and 1-12 present proficiency levels for reading (1998) and math (1996), respectively, for fourth-grade students in high-poverty schools. In nine of the forty states sampled for reading, at least 75 percent of students in high-poverty schools scored below the basic level, and at least 50 percent in thirty-seven states scored below the basic level. Fifteen percent or more of students in high-poverty schools achieved reading scores at the proficient or advanced level in only five states (figure 1-11). The pattern was somewhat less skewed for math. In twenty-five of the forty-three states sampled, fewer than half the students in high-poverty schools scored at or above the basic level in math. Twenty percent or more of fourth graders in high-poverty schools scored at the proficient or advanced level in math in only five states (figure 1-12). In addition to the generally low levels of performance in those skills tests by students in high-poverty schools, the data show great variation among the states in levels of proficiency.

Policies, Programs, and Funding

Achievement levels in schools where children from low-income families are concentrated are on average lower than in schools where most children are from families with higher incomes. The predominant view in the mid-1960s was that such differences in average levels of achievement were attributable primarily to differences in resources devoted to schooling. At that time local governments raised most of the revenue to support elementary and secondary schooling. Additional funding from the federal government to provide more resources for schools in low-income areas—the main initial emphasis of Title I—was regarded as key to improving performance of children in those low-income schools and to narrowing gaps in achievement.

Federal policy officials made efforts from the beginning of Title I to monitor the program, evaluate its performance, and make modifications intended to improve it. Many of the earliest efforts were intended to ensure that a disproportionate share of the funds went to schools with concentrations of children from low-income families and to tighten specifications for programs and monitoring of activities supported by Title I funds. When concerns arose about the efficacy of the program in raising

Figure 1-11 Fourth-Grade Reading Skills in High-Poverty Schools by State, 1998

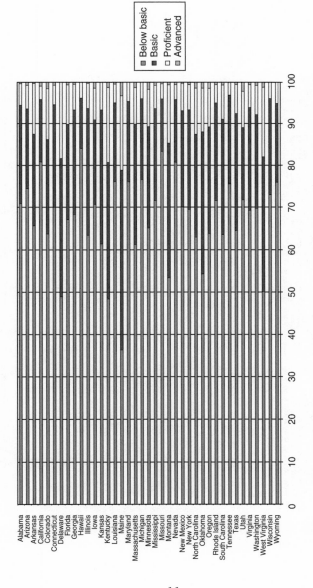

Below basic
Basic
Proficient
Advanced

NOTE: *High-poverty schools* are defined as those with more than 75 percent of students eligible for subsidized lunches.

SOURCE: Authors' calculations using state NAEP restricted data for fourth-grade reading, 1998.

11

Figure 1-12 Fourth-Grade Math Skills in High-Poverty Schools by State, 1996

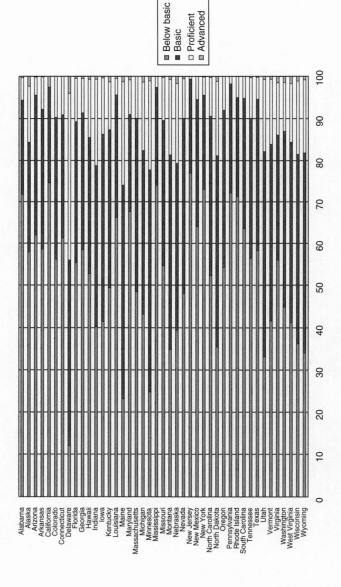

NOTE: *High-poverty schools* are defined as those with more than 75 percent of students eligible for subsidized lunches.

SOURCE: Authors' calculations using state NAEP restricted data for fourth-grade math, 1996.

achievement levels of children from low-income and minority families, efforts to tighten the administration of the program typically intensified.

Several developments raised more fundamental questions, however. First, a gradual accumulation of evidence from studies of the effects of Title I failed to show any measurable improvement for children served by the program. In addition, broad measures of achievement, such as NAEP test scores, showed no continuing improvement in relative achievement of students from low-income and minority schools during the late 1980s and the 1990s. The presumed linkage between funding and achievement was increasingly questioned. Although state programs increasingly narrowed differences in resources available to schools in low- and high-income areas, no concomitant convergence in achievement resulted. Those circumstances raised questions about the extent to which simply providing additional funds and monitoring their expenditure could compensate for whatever factors were primarily responsible for low achievement of children in low-income and minority schools.

The main focus of policy—at least during the first decade of Title I— was improving evaluation and developing more detailed rules for administering the program. That emphasis was accompanied by efforts to identify specific approaches or practices that might improve performance. When the enabling legislation was reauthorized on roughly a five-year cycle, limited changes that influenced implementation of the program were often enacted. The 1994 reauthorization introduced more thoroughgoing changes by encouraging the use of Title I funds for schoolwide programs.[10] That change was a culmination of a shift in the emphasis of policy from specified treatments for specific children who were identified to participate in Title I programs toward efforts to raise the performance of all students in schools with high concentrations of children from low-income families and with low average achievement.

The No Child Left Behind Act of 2001 (signed into law in January 2002) carried the shift a step further.[11] The legislation strengthened requirements for state standards and for testing to see that achievement standards were met and required that adequate progress was made each year toward meeting the standards. States received more flexibility across different categories of federal funds and across different kinds of compensatory programs.

The new legislation also provided for remedial actions should schools fail to meet standards or make progress toward achieving them, and it expanded the range of choices available for compensatory programs. For students in persistently failing schools, for example, low-income students with deficient achievement could use Title I funds to obtain supplemental services (such as tutoring) from either the public or the private sector. The significance of some changes will depend on details of their implementation that the federal government, the states, and local school systems must arrange jointly.

Title I provides funds that flow through states to local school districts.[12] The federal government computes the initial Title I allocations to school districts; states administer the allocations to districts and schools based on federal formulas. During most of the 1970s and 1980s, the way that schools were required to account for Title I funds encouraged the use of those funds to employ additional instructional staff and to provide supplementary teaching and tutoring services for children specifically identified to participate in the program. During the 1990s, however, the emphasis shifted toward improving performance for schools as a whole.

Reauthorization legislation made it easier for schools with more than a threshold percentage of students in poverty to use Title I funds to benefit all students through schoolwide programs. In many schools Title I now provides "flexible funding that may be used for supplementary instruction, professional development, new computers, after-school programs, and other strategies for student achievement" (DOE, PES 2001a, 9). Expenditure patterns reported for 1997–1998 show more than three-fourths of Title I funds devoted to instruction: approximately equal numbers of additional teachers and aides accounted for most expenditures. The pattern does not differ appreciably from patterns reported when pullout programs were more prevalent.[13]

Title I funds initially amounted to $4 billion–5 billion per year (in 2001 dollars). Funding increased unevenly to nearly $9 billion in 2001. Because the number of children in elementary and secondary schools has increased since the late 1960s, the increase in funding per student was somewhat smaller. The distribution of funds is skewed toward school districts with high concentrations of children from poor families, of course, and within those districts toward high-poverty schools. Within schools, in turn, children with low achievement are targeted, either for participation in special supplemental programs or for meeting higher standards in schoolwide programs. In addition elementary schools get a larger share of Title I funds than junior-high grades or secondary schools.[14] Consequently the typical beneficiary receives much more additional resources from Title I than would be suggested by comparing funds from Title I with the total budget (from all sources) for elementary and secondary schooling.

Although federal Title I funds have recently accounted for only about 2 percent of the total budget from all sources for elementary and secondary schools, the additional resources available to children who benefit from Title I is much more consequential than the comparison suggests. In 1997–1998, for example, average Title I funding per poor student was $495 in elementary schools and $372 in secondary schools.[15] The funds added about 13 percent to school-level personnel expenditures per low-income child in elementary schools and about 7 percent in secondary schools. Title I funds added 12 percent to personnel expenditures per low-income student in schools with schoolwide programs, 16 percent per low-income student in targeted assistance schools, and 25 percent per Title I participant.[16] For children needing assistance in high-poverty schools with schoolwide programs and for Title I participants in targeted assistance schools, federal Title I funds accounted for a significant addition to available resources. Those additional funds are sufficient to have made a noticeable contribution to achievement if Title I matters.

The Rest of the Study

In chapter 2 we discuss the history of changes in Title I policy. In chapter 3 we review evaluations and summaries of quantitative studies of the effects of Title I on achievement. In chapter 4 we present new evidence on the relationship between Title I and student achievement in recent years. We then summarize our conclusions in chapter 5.

As is apparent from readily available test score information, achievement levels of poor and minority children are well below those of other children. In addition the achievement gaps that motivated enactment of Title I, after narrowing during the 1970s and early 1980s, have shown no further improvement during at least the past decade and a half. Those patterns raise serious questions about whether Title I has significantly contributed to bringing up the achievement of poor and minority children toward levels of achievement reached by other children. Any possible contribution that Title I was making to improving achievement does not seem to have been reflected by a noticeable reduction in the achievement gap for poor and minority children for more than a decade.

The analyses that we discuss in this book examine whether Title I has been meeting the more limited goal of improving achievement of beneficiaries of the program. If elimination, or at least significant reduction, of achievement gaps is an unrealistic goal, the program might nevertheless be making a worthwhile contribution if significant improvement in achievement could be traced to participation in Title I. On the basis of our analysis of achievement levels reached by children who participated in Title I programs, we conclude that the program has not produced systematic, significant improvements in achievement. That is, children who received services funded by Title I did not generally perform significantly better in achievement tests than children who did not. For such comparisons, differences in characteristics of children and their schools were taken into account by statistical and other means to ensure, as much as possible, that the effects of Title I participation were examined for similar children in similar school circumstances.

We base our judgments about the effects of Title I on the many studies carried out over more than thirty years. Those studies used a variety of methods to examine data on achievement and the impact of Title I. Although some estimates in some studies indicated that Title I participation was making a positive impact on achievement, negative estimated effects in many of those same studies and in other studies indicated negative Title I effects. The typical pattern for results reported in the studies that we discuss, as well as for our own analyses, is some positive and some negative estimates of the impact of Title I. That pattern applies to analyses that examined Title I effects in earlier years and in more recent years after a new and different rationale for Title I policies had been developed and the implementation of the program had been significantly reformed.

2

A Review of Title I Policy

In several important ways the enactment of Title I represented a departure in federal education policy. It authorized the first broad infusion of federal funds to support elementary and secondary schooling. It provided for the distribution of funds through states and local political units to schools with disproportionate numbers of children from poor families. The program aimed at raising average achievement in low-income schools toward levels realized in higher-income schools with presumably more available resources to support educational performance. As a major new compensatory education program, Title I was not patterned after smaller programs or pilot efforts with demonstrated success. State and local agencies without experience in distributing such funds administered the Title I grants; school administrators without insights from experience regarding the kinds of programs or resources that could be expected to produce improved achievement made the decisions on spending the funds.[1]

Implementing the New Program

The states received federal funds under Title I as grants and then distributed the funds to local education agencies (LEAs). The amounts distributed were calculated as 50 percent of the average expenditure per school child in each state, multiplied by the number of five- to seventeen-year-olds in the school district from low-income families.[2] Low-income status was initially defined as annual family income less than $2,000. Children in families receiving welfare payments (under Aid to Families with Dependent Children, AFDC) were counted even if their incomes exceeded the threshold (*Congressional Quarterly Almanac* 1965,

275–76). Title I grants could not exceed 30 percent of an LEA's budget, and availability was limited to districts with at least a minimum of eligible students. By the 1968–1969 school year about 9 million children took part in Title I programs, and almost 60 percent of the nation's 27,000 school districts received some money (*National Journal* 1969, 124).

The commissioner of education, an office in the cabinet-level Department of Health, Education, and Welfare, had federal responsibility for the program. States were responsible for ensuring that Title I funds were used for programs to benefit educationally deprived children as mandated. The states were also responsible for making sure that administration of the funds used appropriate accounting procedures and fiscal controls, with periodic reports to evaluate the effectiveness of the program. The federal Office of Education computed allocations by county; state education agencies allotted grants to local school districts and approved their plans for specific programs. The legislation did not spell out the kinds of services for poor children or the activities and programs of schools that were eligible for support: local districts had great flexibility on spending the funds (*Congressional Quarterly Almanac* 1965, 276–77).

Expectations of Title I were high.[3] Poor performance of children from low-income families in the target schools was regarded as attributable primarily to insufficient resources for adequate instruction. Consequently the key remedy was viewed as augmenting the resources available to those schools. Deference to local decisions on how the money should be spent was consistent with the viewing of funding as the main problem, rather than an absence of constructive opportunities to improve children's achievement. As an antipoverty strategy, breaking into the cycle by supplementing the resources available to schools otherwise unable to match the expenditures of more affluent schools was seen as a strategy for reducing self-perpetuation of poverty across generations.

By the end of the 1960s the administration and the performance of Title I were garnering increased criticism. Evaluations of the effects of Title I on achievement (a state responsibility) were generally superficial and uneven and provided little evidence of improvement for poor children. One line of criticism was that funds were not benefiting the right children because formulas were outdated or because funds were spread too thinly over too many schools and too many children. From the out-set the formula for allocation of Title I money stirred controversy.

Another line of criticism was that the funds were being spent inap-propriately on systemwide programs, on supplies, on higher salaries, and on more amenities for teachers and administrators. Better state and local safeguards against such misdirection of Title I funds were viewed as the appropriate remedy (*National Journal* 1969, 124; Jennings 2000, 518). Because Title I was still quite new at that point, it was thought that more careful evaluation might demonstrate its efficacy or that correction of any shortcomings in administration might improve its performance.

The 1970s

The transition to the 1970s was marked by the accumulation of some initial experience introducing and running Title I and by the beginning of a Republican presidency. In addition to emerging criticism about the administration of Title I funds and the performance of Title I programs and a Republican emphasis on converting categorical grants to block grants, fiscal reasons for limiting growth in appropriations became more pressing (*Congressional Quarterly Almanac* 1967, 611). Arguing that the Democratic Congress wanted to spend too much money in an inflation-ary time, President Richard Nixon vetoed the education bill appropriat-ing funds for Title I in August 1970. Congress, however, overrode his veto (*Congressional Quarterly Almanac* 1970, 266).

To ensure that Title I funds were spent according to congressional intent, a new comparability requirement was introduced so that school districts would spend as much per pupil in Title I schools as in schools not receiving Title I. Similarly, "supplement, not supplant" requirements were imposed for resources that poor children would have received in the absence of Title I money (Jennings 2000, 518; Congress 1987, 5–9). The emphasis on identifiable services for specifically designated educa-tionally deprived children—services that fiscal audits could readily verify—encouraged the widespread use of pullout programs, in which recipients of Title I services were pulled out of regular classes for special instruction or tutoring. In general the 1970s began with a tightening of administration of Title I and limited growth in appropriations for the program.

From the beginning, one of the most controversial elements of Title I was the federal formula for allocating the funds. Pronounced shifts in funding produced by the original formula led to significant changes under the 1974 amendments. Inflation in the late 1960s and early 1970s had contributed to pushing up nominal incomes; consequently a declining proportion of all families with children remained below the $2,000 family-income threshold in the formula. Data from the 1970 census showed a large reduction in the number of children in families with incomes below $2,000.[4] The formula for distributing Title I funds included families receiving AFDC payments even if their incomes exceeded $2,000; as a consequence AFDC families accounted for a growing share of families in the distribution formula. The AFDC component of children in the formula, for example, increased from about 10 percent in 1966 to more than 22 percent in 1969; by 1974, children of AFDC recipients were the dominant group in the allocation formula. The allocation of Title I funds was increasingly shifting toward states with high AFDC payments and participation (Congress 1987, 14; HEW 1969, 6).

The 1974 amendments changed both the low-income threshold and the AFDC components of the allocation formula. The official poverty line used to compile the 1970 census data became the new income cutoff, and children in families receiving AFDC payments that brought incomes above that level were given a two-thirds weighting in the formula. The hold-harmless provision for local education agencies was set at 85 percent of the previous year's allocation. An adjustment for cost differences among states was reduced from 50 percent of the greater of state or national average per pupil spending to 40 percent of the state level, with limits set at 20 percent above or below the national average (Congress 1987, 14).

The 1978 amendments allowed schools with 75 percent or more of their children from low-income families to use Title I funds to implement schoolwide programs. Many of the usual restrictions on uses of Title I funds were not imposed on schools choosing that approach. Because funds from state or local sources had to match the Title I funds in schoolwide programs, schoolwide programs were implemented in only a few cases during the next few years.[5]

The federal formula for Title I basic grants was modified again in 1978 to account fully for children in AFDC families. A special variant of the formula, however, was used to allocate half the appropriations exceeding those for fiscal year 1979. In addition to the basic grants, legislation provided for incentive grants to match state spending on compensatory programs and concentration grants for counties with especially high concentrations of children from low-income families. No money, however, was ever appropriated for the former, and the latter often received no funding (Congress 1987, 14). Various provisions to foster greater accountability, to carry out studies to evaluate the program, and to make previous administrative regulations into legislative requirements were enacted into law with each new set of amendments.

The 1980s and 1990s

Several developments seem to have contributed to a gradual loss of confidence in Title I as originally conceived. By the 1980s the achievement levels of most children receiving Title I services remained well below those of children from higher-income families. That result occurred despite the fact that the bulk of the funds were allocated to schools with high concentrations of children from low-income families. Criticizing the performance of the program on the basis of its targeting became more difficult. Because the administration of auditing procedures to ensure accountability had matured, more detailed or stringent regulation would achieve little. The procedures were intended to ensure (1) maintenance of effort for funding from state and local sources, (2) comparability of nonfederal funding levels in schools that received Title I funds and those that did not, and (3) augmentation requirements for Title I funds to be used to supplement, not supplant, other resources.

The widespread practice of hiring special aides to pull out children from their regular classrooms enabled schools to demonstrate that they were using Title I funds according to congressional intent as interpreted by the Department of Education although the effectiveness of that practice was not established. No other practices had been identified as consistently and reliably effective in improving children's performance. By the mid-1980s, evidence from careful research on the effects of Title I failed to demonstrate that Title I was making a significant contribution to reducing the achievement gap for children from low-income families.

In addition to doubts about what might be expected from Title I, concerns about the general performance of the public school system were growing. The Reagan administration's Department of Education publicized those concerns in *A Nation at Risk*. In the 1980s emphasis began to shift somewhat away from fiscal accountability and the provision of separate, identifiable services to disadvantaged children. Increased attention was focused on levels of achievement of children eligible for Title I in relation to goals for academic achievement for all students. The shift from monitoring inputs toward more attention to output expected from schools was exemplified by the Bush administration's policies in the late 1980s. Those policies focused on national goals for achievement, along with efforts to meet the goals by the end of the century. By 1994 Congress passed the Goals 2000 bill that continued a broad emphasis on achieving academic standards in the nation's elementary and secondary schools (Jennings 2000, 519–20).

When reauthorization was on the congressional agenda in 1981, the Elementary and Secondary Education Act was criticized on the grounds that "it was too long, too detailed, and too inflexible, and that it stifled creativity and initiative on the part of local educators" (Congress, 1987, 19). The 1981 amendments continued Title I as a categorical program, however, despite the Reagan administration's proposal to consolidate all federal support for elementary and secondary education into a block grant that could be used at the discretion of state and local governments.[6] Some requirements for administration and implementation were loosened, but provisions enacted in 1978 to allow schoolwide projects in schools with 75 percent or more of their children from poor families were deleted. Authority for schoolwide programs was restored in 1983.

Regarding regulatory requirements, particularly those focused on identifiable services devoted to specific children, schoolwide programs introduced a great deal of regulatory flexibility. Title I funds allocated to schools with disproportionate concentrations of children from low-income families could be used to improve academic achievement in such schools for the student body as a whole. The focus for accountability was shifted accordingly from fiscal audits of inputs and their uses to a greater attention to meeting achievement standards. Achievement goals were emphasized not only for children with the most serious academic deficiencies but for all students in schools where a pattern of poor achievement and low expectations was typical.

The use of schoolwide programs expanded during the late 1980s and the 1990s and became widespread after the 1994 amendments that reduced the threshold for eligibility from schools with 75 percent of children from low-income families to schools with 50 percent (with an intermediate eligibility threshold of 60 percent for 1995–1996) (Riddle 1994, 27).[7] Earlier changes, such as removal of the matching requirement in 1988, also stimulated broader introduction of schoolwide programs. The number of schools operating under schoolwide plan authority increased from 621 in 1989–1990 to 2,069 in 1991–1992. In 1992 the relaxation of the special fiscal requirement that nonfederal funds be at least 100 percent of the previous year's budget level to 90 percent encouraged schoolwide projects as well (Riddle 1992, 44–45).

By the late 1990s, discussions on the role of Title I concentrated on the concept of standards-based reform—the idea that challenging standards should be set and educational strategies should be designed to help all students achieve them. In that context Title I was no longer seen as a program providing specific compensatory services to children with low academic achievement in schools with high concentrations of children from low-income families. Instead Title I was seen as a funding source to help such schools set higher standards and help all students perform better.

The conceptual transformation shifted the emphasis in discussions of evaluation to issues such as whether funds were targeted primarily to schools with high concentrations of children from low-income families and whether schools were working to integrate Title I resources into regular academic programs to achieve more challenging standards. In

1997–1998, 58 percent of all public schools in the country (95 percent of schools with 75 percent or more of its students from poor families) received Title I funding compared with 62 percent of all schools in 1993–1994. And in 1997–1998, more than 16,000 of the schools receiving Title I funds operated schoolwide programs compared with 4,600 in 1994–1995 (DOE, PES 1999, 8–11). The transformation of Title I was intended to further what the Department of Education described as its central objective: "To support state and local efforts to help *all* children reach challenging standards by providing additional resources to schools and students who have farthest to go in achieving the goal" (Riddle 1992, 44–45).

Current Policy

The No Child Left Behind Act of 2001 most recently reauthorized Title I.[8] In many respects the new law builds on and extends policies emphasized in the 1994 reauthorization under the Improving America's Schools Act. Reducing the poverty threshold from 50 to 40 percent, for example, further encouraged the introduction of schoolwide Title I programs. Other features of the new legislation followed and extended earlier policy approaches: identification of schools that failed to perform adequately and an emphasis on the need to improve performance. As with the 1994 reauthorization, states had a major role in implementing the new policies. Several themes of Title I policy have shown considerable continuity over the years; many elements of policies widely publicized as new in 1994, such as schoolwide programs, really extended or gave new emphasis to policies introduced earlier.

The national political leadership has promoted the view that new features of the No Child Left Behind Act can be expected to improve Title I performance and has publicized some features as departures from previous policies. Goals that states set for failing schools are quite explicit. They must be met within twelve years; criteria for "adequate yearly progress" must be established in that context. Yearly math and reading tests are required for grades three through eight to monitor progress. More significant perhaps, test results must be reported for each school, as well as separately for groups defined by race, ethnicity, income, English proficiency, and disability status.

The most important new elements in the 2001 Title I legislation, however, provided some limited opportunities for parents to make decisions about remedies for their children enrolled in failing schools. Children in Title I schools targeted for improvement could transfer to higher-performing public schools in the same district, and school districts would be required to use Title I funds to pay transportation costs for students who transferred. Title I funds could be used to pay for supplemental services (services, such as tutoring, that can be obtained from either public or private sources) for children with low achievement from low-income families in schools that failed to show enough improvement. In both cases school districts establish the range of options for choices available to parents. Nevertheless, under the new legislation, parents would be provided with more information about school performance and would have at least a limited range of choices about schools and services for their children. The new elements in Title I policy build on and extend policy approaches introduced in earlier, periodic reauthorizations.

Title I Resources

The amount of resources that has historically been devoted to the program is an important aspect of Title I. In nominal dollars the budget for Title I increased from about $1 billion in 1966 to about $8 billion in 2000. After adjustment for inflation, total real resources funded by the program went up about 83 percent for that period. But because the number of school-age children increased, real resources per child increased by about 68 percent. Over the same period total real resources from all sources per student in elementary and secondary schools more than doubled (Hanushek 1991, 11–12).

Figure 2-1 shows the trend in total Title I grants to school districts. The uneven pattern of growth is much more evident when Title I funding is expressed in constant dollars than in current dollars. Constant dollars—after adjustment for inflation—reveal a period of growth in the

Figure 2-1 Title I LEA Grant Allocation History, FY 1966–2001

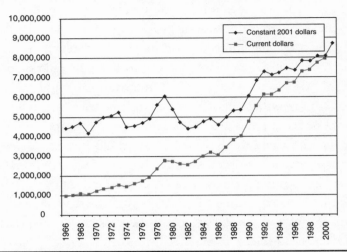

NOTE: Constant-dollar measures are obtained by using chain-type price indexes for personal consumption expenditures in the gross domestic product. Department of Commerce, Bureau of Economic Analysis.

SOURCE: Department of Education, Office of Compensatory Education Programs and Title I.

late 1970s followed by decline in the first part of the 1980s. Strong growth in the early 1990s was followed by more subdued growth during the rest of the decade. The trend of Title I funding per pupil, reported in constant and current dollars in figure 2-2, shows a pattern fairly similar to that for total funding because elementary school enrollment recorded only a slight increase. Real Title I funding per elementary school pupil is a useful index of resources potentially available to children but is not a measure of resources that each participant actually receives.[9]

Although the Nixon administration did not favor categorical programs such as Title I, real resources devoted to the program were not cut back sharply during the early 1970s. By the mid-1970s real funding was at about the same level as in 1970, primarily because rising inflation eroded small nominal gains. But funding was temporarily higher under the Carter administration before being cut back significantly under the Reagan administration in the early 1980s. A decline in the number of

Figure 2-2 Title I Funding per Pupil, 1966–2001

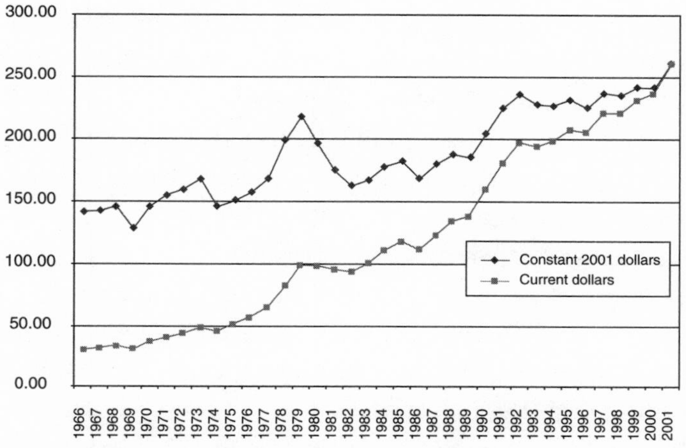

NOTE: Constant-dollar measures are obtained by using chain-type price indexes for personal consumption expenditures in the gross domestic product. Department of Commerce, Bureau of Economic Analysis.

SOURCE: Department of Education, Office of Compensatory Education Programs and Title I.

elementary school children in the first part of the 1980s mitigated, but did not entirely offset, the decline in real resources. The exceptionally strong growth in real resources during the Bush administration in 1989–1992 was followed by more modest growth during the Clinton administration. The amount of real resources per student increased especially rapidly in the late 1980s, but the growing number of elementary school students almost completely offset increases in real resources during most of the 1990s. In contrast to that stability, appropriations for Title I increased by about 18 percent in 2002 and 13 percent in 2003; a further increase of about 6 percent (to $12.35 billion) was requested for 2004.

Title I funds were, of course, unevenly distributed to students. In the early 1990s, an estimated 6 million children participated in Title I annually, compared with some 42 million children in elementary and secondary schools combined. Participation was uneven by grade level, with Title I programs in three-fourths of all elementary schools, one-half of middle and junior high schools, and one-quarter of high schools. Participation was more uneven for the students in those schools: about 20 percent of children in the first and third grades received Title I services compared with 5 to 8 percent of students in the seventh grade. And participation varied by the extent of poverty in schools. According to Prospects data, about 32 percent of third-grade children in high-poverty schools (with at least 75 percent of students eligible for subsidized lunch) received Title I services compared with 12 percent in all schools taken together and 4 percent of children in low-poverty schools (with less than 25 percent of students eligible for subsidized lunch). The estimates were made when schoolwide programs accounted for a minuscule fraction of children (Puma et al. 1997, 2–11; DOE, OUS 1996, 13–14).

Following the 1994 amendments that encouraged widespread use of schoolwide Title I programs, participation in Title I programs increasingly involved the whole school instead of specific children identified as participants. In general, however, funds apparently became targeted more strongly toward schools with higher proportions of children from poverty-level families. By 1997–1998, 95 percent of high-poverty schools received Title I funds compared with 79 percent in 1993–1994. By the late 1990s, school districts in the highest-poverty quartile were receiving 49 percent of all Title I funds. Most of the increase in funding concentration since the early 1990s was a result of more targeting of schools within school districts; the formulas for allocating Title I funds among school districts were not substantially changed (DOE, PES 1999, 75–77).[10] Although poverty levels figure prominently in the allocation of funds among school districts and schools, the services supported by those funds have traditionally been provided to children on the basis of deficiencies in achievement instead of the poverty level of their families. Since the mid-1990s, Title I services have been provided on that basis for targeted assistance schools, but individual students are not typically singled out for separate treatment under schoolwide programs.

3

A Review of Title I Evaluations

The legislation establishing Title I in 1965 considered the evaluation of Title I's performance important (McLaughlin 1975, 1–15). This chapter summarizes and discusses the most important of the many studies of the program's effects. Over time weaknesses in earlier studies' methodology have been identified, new data and analytical techniques have been developed, and more sophisticated studies have resulted. Nevertheless answers to important questions about the performance of Title I remain somewhat inconclusive. Reports on early evaluative studies of Title I share a disappointment that the evidence has not shown systematic improvements in the achievement levels of children receiving Title I services, as well as hopeful anticipation that improvements in the program itself or in data and methods used for evaluation might show more promising results (McLaughlin 1975, 17–32; Wargo et al. 1972).

Despite a strong emphasis on evaluation from the outset of the program, differences arose about measures of performance to be used in evaluation and about how evaluation results would be useful or influential.[1] Regarding measures of performance, some lawmakers wanted to ensure that the funding particularly benefited children from poor families, especially minority children and those living in poor areas. The consideration of a sufficiently broad distribution to generate and maintain political support for the program was somewhat at odds with the concern for relatively narrow targeting, however. As a result the formulas that determined the distribution of funds to constituencies always received attention.

Evaluation also focused on the impact on academic achievement, perhaps because the strongest element in the rationale for the program came from the recognition that the achievement of children in poor families fell behind children in more affluent families. The evaluation of student performance was also based on the expectation that funds for more educational resources for those children would help close the achievement gap. The examination of the impact on achievement was almost always a major focus of efforts to evaluate Title I, and achievement is likewise the main emphasis in this review.

The most prevalent concept of evaluation, at least among social scientists and policy analysts, involves the examination of the benefits and costs of policies and an assessment of whether taxpayers and beneficiaries are getting their money's worth. According to the predominant view, the results of evaluation could aid in decisionmaking about modifying program design and adjusting levels and composition of budgets to improve performance. Schools of public policy and policy offices of federal agencies in the mid-1960s favored that view; it remains influential.

Other views about the uses of evaluation focused less on administrative and management processes and emphasized influence through political channels. Political influence might make itself felt through a kind of adversarial proceeding in the marketplace of opinion. Alternatively, parental pressures might stimulate policy changes on the basis of evaluative information given to them. Precisely how such influences might work their way through the system to improve performance was usually not spelled out; scant information on the efficacy of those alternative approaches was available.

Since the enactment of the Elementary and Secondary Education Act in 1965, two major congressionally mandated national studies have emerged: *The Sustaining Effects Study* and *Prospects: The Congressionally Mandated Study of Educational Growth and Opportunity*.[2] Those studies include major data collection efforts. Data for *Sustaining Effects* were gathered from 1976 through 1979; for *Prospects,* about fifteen years later. Many other research efforts were more varied in their approaches and often limited their scope.[3] Several of those studies took place before the two major national data collection and evaluation projects. We begin with a review of those studies.

The Early Studies

Title I has often been characterized as a funding mechanism instead of a well-defined program because of the considerable discretion by local education agencies and schools in determining program services, particularly in the early years (Vinovskis 1999, 189). In addition guidelines for evaluation by the states initially lacked detail and rigor. Annual evaluation was mandated by federal legislation, but state and local agencies were ill equipped to respond by conducting careful evaluations. In part the difficulty resulted because Title I was a new program and the first significant foray into federal funding of elementary and secondary schooling, historically the responsibility of local governments. Sensitivity to fears that federal funding would be accompanied by the imposition of extensive federal control apparently contributed to a reluctance at the federal level to press too hard for serious evaluation. And, of course, evaluations that showed unfavorable results always threatened those responsible for administering the program, as well as the funding itself. The real difficulties encountered in developing definitive evaluations were not fully appreciated at that time. Nevertheless, increasingly ambitious efforts at the federal level to carry out useful evaluations began in the late 1960s.

Because evidence about the performance of a major new program is inevitably limited at the outset, Milbrey W. McLaughlin's (1975, 22) characterization of the first two annual reports as "emphasizing impressionistic local reports, testimonial data, and photojournalism" is not surprising. The available evidence was piecemeal, unrepresentative of the nation as a whole, or subject to other shortcomings. Perhaps understandably program administrators were reluctant to grapple with unfavorable evidence. McLaughlin quotes from a review by Robert Dentler, Center for Urban Education, of the second annual report on Title I, published in the summer of 1968:

> I became fascinated with that part of the report that evaluates the effects of Title I in big cities, because of the great difference between its conclusions and the conclusions one might reach from reading

the more than 60 Title I evaluations prepared by CUE since 1966. The federal report is, with cautions, a success story. The Center reports document a series of earnest attempts and invite impression of cumulative failure. (22)

Dentler considered the optimistic official report seriously at odds with his assessment based on studies by CUE.

Federal officials responsible for the evaluation of Title I recognized the necessity of taking the lead in developing systematic evidence on effectiveness to be used to shape policy for the nation. In 1967 the TEMPO division of the General Electric Company was commissioned to study the impact of Title I on achievement. The study examined experiences in eleven districts with programs that seemed successful to determine the features of participating pupils and programs. Data for the study were obtained from "11 school districts chosen for analysis because there was reason to believe that successful compensatory programs were in operation in at least some of the schools" (McLaughlin 1975, 36). Analysts examined experience in five districts in greater detail.

The results disappointed analysts anticipating evidence of positive effects on achievement, especially in light of the selectivity of the sample. In his summary of the results, Joseph Wholey, one of the senior federal government policy analysts, made two points about the evaluation of cost-effectiveness: "There appears to have been a very slight decline in average pupil achievement in the Title I schools studied . . . . On the other hand, there appears to have been a slight improvement in achievement of the lowest 10 percent of the pupils in the schools studied" (ibid.). The Office of Education's report to Congress presented the report's conclusions in a somewhat understated form.

In 1968 and 1969 some special surveys occurred that were likely more representative of schools with Title I programs than the TEMPO study. Nonetheless they reported similar results. The report on the 1968 survey describes the impact of Title I: "For participating and nonparticipating pupils, the rate of progress in reading skills kept pace with their historical rate of progress. Pupils taking part in compensatory reading programs were not progressing fast enough to allow them to catch up to nonparticipating students" (McLaughlin 1975, 59). The conclusions of the OOE report based on the 1969 survey were similar, according to McLaughlin (1975, 61):

> Participants in reading programs for the disadvantaged had lower pretest scores and post-test scores than nonparticipants. It would appear that the compensatory programs were indeed reaching those who needed special help in reading. Negative gains scores for most "participating" groups in all grades seem to indicate that even when a lower "starting point" is considered, participants progressed at a slower rate than nonparticipants.

The Office of Education essentially never disseminated the latter report. In their reanalysis and synthesis of evaluation data through 1970, Michael Wargo and his associates emphasized in their summary of the studies based on 1968 and 1969 data that *"participants gained less than nonparticipants and consequently fell further behind their nonparticipating peers and national norms"* (Wargo et al. 1972, 8).

Those studies, like others undertaken at the time such as the Coleman report (Coleman et al. 1966) and the report of the Civil Rights Commission (U.S. Commission on Civil Rights 1967), found virtually no evidence that participation in compensatory education—Title I and other programs—resulted in gains in achievement (McLaughlin 1975, 35, 67). But the difficulty in obtaining useful achievement data introduced uncertainty about the validity of the results. The relevance of the results also raised questions because some analysts did not regard achievement effects as the only relevant measure of effectiveness. Nevertheless, achievement measures continued as the main focus of evaluation efforts. Development of the NAEP program was getting underway at the time, and various other approaches were being taken to examine the effect of Title I on achievement. By the mid-1970s Congress mandated a study that included an ambitious effort at data collection focused on achievement.[4]

A strategy intermittently pursued looked at local Title I programs that were generally regarded as successful to discover what features of a program contributed to successful performance, instead of trying to measure the contribution of Title I to achievement. In one such effort analysts reviewed state evaluation reports to find exemplary local Title I projects. According to state reports on those local projects describing their performance in subjective terms, a positive relationship existed between expenditures and benefits in most cases. But "five of the six reports that presented empirical evidence to support their conclusion found no positive relationship between Title I project expenditures and cognitive benefits" (Wargo et al. 1972, 9). Another effort identified forty-one local compensatory education projects that seemed to raise achievement levels; case studies on the projects were published in an "It Works!" series. Unfortunately follow-up studies carried out by the same research organization found that the erstwhile successful programs no longer appeared to be working (McLaughlin 1975, 88).

The many studies of various compensatory education programs in the late 1960s and early 1970s exhibit great variation in their goals, methods, and reliability. Stephen Mullin and Anita Summers (1983, 339–47) examined the results of forty-seven studies of different compensatory programs and syntheses selected with the following guidelines: (1) the studies addressed compensatory education, achievement, or cost-effectiveness and (2) the studies met at least some minimal standards of evaluation techniques, representativeness of the sample, explicit achievement measures, and attention to program costs. Many studies of compensatory education reviewed were studies of Title I programs. The general conclusions of the studies, as described by Mullin and Summers (ibid., 340), were that "the majority of the 47 studies surveyed support the general conclusion that compensatory education programs have a small but positive effect on the achievement growth of disadvantaged students." But based on their analysis, they added, "This optimistic conclusion is an overstatement of the realities, however" (ibid., 342). They then discussed the implications of sources of bias and other shortcomings of the studies reviewed.

Regarding the cost-effectiveness of Title I programs, Mullin and Summers (ibid., 342) concluded that "no significant association can be found between dollars spent and achievement gains. No approach and no program characteristic was consistently found to be effective." One possible conclusion from reports available on the results of research by the mid-1970s was that Title I had little or no effect on the achievement of pupils served by the program. Another possible conclusion, however, was that available data and analytic methods were not adequate to develop conclusive results. In that case a carefully developed national study might help to clarify the impact.

Sustaining Effects Study

The congressionally mandated Sustaining Effects Study funded by the U.S. Department of Education began in 1975 with a systematic data collection effort involving "as many as 120,000 pupils in a representative sample of over 300 elementary schools throughout the country for three successive school years, starting with the 1976–1977 school year. Three additional years were devoted to analyzing and reporting the results" (Carter 1984, 4). The study was characterized as "the largest study ever undertaken of elementary education" and "the largest and most comprehensive evaluation of the effectiveness of Title I ever undertaken" (ibid., 4, 6).

Analyzing the effects of Title I on achievement was a major goal of that national study. Achievement tests in literacy, reading, and math were administered in the fall and in the spring for three consecutive years. Student attitudes were also assessed, and teachers reported on the kinds and amount of instruction that children received. The study included four other areas: a detailed examination of students in a sample of high-poverty schools; analysis of economic status, socioeconomic characteristics, and attitudes of parents; examination of the costs and educational effectiveness of different kinds of activities; and the effects of summer programs on achievement. Twenty individual reports described and summarized the studies and their results (ibid., 13).

For much of the analysis, students were divided into three categories: (1) Title I students (those reported by schools as recipients of Title I services); (2) needy students with which Title I students could be compared (reported by teachers as needing Title I services but not receiving them); and (3) regular students (those identified as not needing

Title I services and not receiving them). According to Launor Carter, "Statistical analysis showed significant gains for Title I students, relative to needy students," for math for grades one through six. "Significant reading gains were found for grades one through three but not for grades four, five, and six." For math "the largest relative gains are in the first grade, and this is also the case for the reading comparisons" (ibid., 6)

His report also notes: "Closer examination shows this improvement to be selective, depending on the level of achievement of the students entering the program. Students entering the program at a near average achievement level profited most from the program, whereas students entering at a low level of achievement seemed to profit little, if at all" (ibid., 11). The gains in achievement from participation in Title I apparently accrued primarily to students who had achieved standardized achievement levels close to the average student before they participated in the program and who were promoted out after only one year. On average, regular students reached noticeably higher achievement standards than participants in Title I. Achievement gains for Title I students that might be attributed to participation in the program were generally small in relation to the gaps in achievement between students in different categories: even the most favorable results showed only a slight contribution to narrowing the achievement gap.

Title I students in the study received services that cost about 35 percent more than what they would have received as regular students (ibid., 5, 11).[5] Although Carter reported that "no demonstrated relationship was found between the costs of the instruction students receive and changes in academic achievement" (5), he noted that the result was controversial because of the possible importance of selection bias. That is, evidence of positive effects might have been diluted if estimated relationships simply reflected that more resources were being spent on children who needed remediation most. Regarding differences in characteristics of services provided under Title I, Carter said, "We had hoped to find some instructional programs that were particularly effective with disadvantaged students, but we did not find them" (12).

The Sustaining Effects Study confirmed the importance of family background characteristics, compared with the effects of schools, as the

Coleman report had also emphasized. Those involved in the research effort became convinced that a more ambitious effort that included panel data would be important to enable them to trace the progress of individual students instead of groups of students over time, and that type of information was an important component of the next major national study.

Prospects Study

In 1988 Congress mandated a national longitudinal study—one that follows individual students over time—to assess the impact of Title I based on a comparison of the "educational achievement of those children with significant participation in Chapter 1 and comparable children who did not receive Chapter 1 services" (Puma et al. 1997, 2). (Originally enacted as Title I of the Elementary and Secondary Education Act in 1965, the program was designated as Chapter 1 in 1981. Its original designation was restored by the 1994 amendments.) Two aspects of the evaluation mandate are noteworthy: (1) the focus of the study was on achievement and (2) the issue was whether Title I services were contributing to improved achievement. The clarity of the mandate seems to have contributed to a more tightly focused study than earlier efforts. The design of the study, the data collected, and the methods used to analyze the data represented a step forward from earlier studies.

Data for the Prospects Study were collected from students, parents, teachers, principals, school district staff, and school records. As a longitudinal study, the main focus was following students. Information was collected from three grade cohorts, beginning in the first, third, and seventh grades. Data for the three cohorts were collected over a three-year period, 1991–1994, and covered a grade span from the first through ninth grades. The sample initially included about 40,000 students from 365 schools. (Because students who moved from their initial schools were followed and interviewed in their new schools, the number of schools involved by the end of the data collection period totaled 1,760.) The scope and detail of the data collected provided an extraordinarily rich body of information for analysis (ibid.).

Data on student achievement (measured, as in the Sustaining Effects Study, on the basis of Comprehensive Tests of Basic Skills, CTBS) generally showed progression from grade to grade for all students, but the starting point for achievement levels of students from high-poverty schools was lower than students from low-poverty schools, national norms, and the sample as a whole. The patterns were similar for different measures of reading and math achievement. In the words of the report: "Children in high-poverty schools began school behind their peers in low-poverty schools. This initial gap in academic achievement remained essentially unchanged as students in high-poverty schools moved into higher grades" (ibid., 25).

When the additional distinction was made of whether students participated in Title I, similar patterns were observed. That is, initial levels of achievement were lower for Title I participants in high-poverty schools as well as in low-poverty schools. Moreover, the gaps remained more or less unchanged as students progressed to higher grade levels. The analysis of the impact of Title I examined whether participation was making any contribution to closing the gap in achievement. Was the rate of progression in achievement significantly affected by Title I participation, so that the gap would be reduced, even if not entirely eliminated? In their efforts to develop an answer, analysts used several statistical approaches, including comparison with a control group of "presumptively eligible" students who were not Title I participants (ibid., 36).[6]

If Title I were reducing the gap, participation would be associated with positive effects on the rate of growth of students' achievement. Estimates of the effects, however, were small and often negative. Statistical controls to reduce the effects of selection bias brought measures of achievement levels closer together, but Title I participation left rates of progression essentially unaffected. In the words of the authors, "After controlling for student, family, and school differences between Chapter 1 participants and nonparticipants, we still find that participants score lower than nonparticipants and that this gap in achievement is *not* closed over time" (ibid., 40, emphasis in the original). The results were basically the same for different measures of achievement, for participation compared with nonparticipation, for different patterns of years of participation, and for comparisons with the control group of nonparticipating students with initial levels of achievement similar to levels of participants.

"What do we conclude from these results?" the authors of the final report asked (ibid., 46).

> Apparently, exposure to school, and general maturation, cause most children to grow over time in their level of achievement. However, where they start has a great deal to do with where they end up relative to other children in their class. Further, Chapter 1 assistance does not reduce the initial gaps in achievement between participating and nonparticipating students.

Those who received Title I services "were clearly in need of supplementary educational assistance. But the services appear to be insufficient to allow them to overcome the relatively large differences between them and their more advantaged classmates" (ibid., 55). The Prospects Study set the high-water mark for careful evaluation of Title I because of its data collection for a representative national sample and application of sophisticated statistical techniques to analyze the results.

The Prospects Study confirmed the findings of the Coleman report and other research that the characteristics of the individual student and his family account for much of the variation in student achievement as measured by test scores. Schools made a difference too, but the effects were smaller than for family background characteristics. The interim report on the Prospects Study (1993) showed that academic standards were much lower in high-poverty schools; performance that rated a C in low-poverty schools was rated at about an A in high-poverty schools (ibid., 12). The focus on schools and their standards in the Prospects Interim Report helped to buttress the case for changes in Title I enacted in the 1994 legislation, such as those encouraging increased use of schoolwide programs.

Promising Results, Continuing Challenges

The 1994 legislation mandated a national assessment of Title I. *Promising Results, Continuing Challenges: The Final Report of the National Assessment of Title I,* published in 1999, gives a useful and thorough description of the program's evolution since 1994. But it retreats from earlier efforts to measure as precisely as possible Title I's contribution to narrowing the achievement gap between children from low-income and high-income families. Instead it describes the shift in the conceptual basis for using Title I financial resources in the mid-1990s and it discusses the effects of Title I on achievement only in general terms based on trends in NAEP scores for high-poverty schools.

The section of the national assessment report on evaluation strategy appears in an appendix. Referring to the 1994 legislation, the report makes the following points about evaluation:

> Because the legislation intended that the Title I program not operate in isolation from the system it is meant to support, progress cannot be evaluated in isolation from state and local reform efforts and results. The National Assessment relied on measures of academic progress overall, as well as state and local assessments. Also, the expansion of schoolwide programs blurred the distinction between program participants and other children. (DOE, NCES, 1999, 189)

Further discussion noted that "control groups are not feasible, nor would they be legal in Title I" (189): apparently all schools were to operate under standards that states were actively promoting and Title I funding was simply intended to help raise achievement in the highest-poverty schools so that all students could meet more stringent state standards (iii).

The report makes only relatively modest claims in statements that suggest a connection between Title I and achievement: "Since 1992, and the reauthorization of Title I, nine-year-olds in the highest-poverty schools gained eight points in NAEP scores, regaining the losses between the late 1980s and early 1990s" (v, 15). The text fails to note what a look at actual NAEP trends shown in their report reveals. The eight-point gain in fourth-grade reading scores from 1992 until 1996 followed a ten-point decline between 1988 to 1992, with the average score for children from high-poverty schools subsequently two points lower in 1996 than eight years earlier (v, exh. 2). From 1992 to 1996, reading scores of fourth-grade children from low-poverty schools increased gradually by eight points. That is, for the 1988–1996 period as a whole, NAEP reading test scores for fourth-grade children from high-poverty schools not only declined but fell farther behind children in low-poverty schools in reading. Math scores likewise showed no trend toward a smaller gap between children from low-poverty and high-poverty schools during a similar time period.[7]

Longitudinal Evaluation of School Change and Performance

The final report that we review, the Longitudinal Evaluation of School Change and Performance (LESCP), was carried out by Westat for the Department of Education and issued in 2001. Data were developed on children's achievement, on teachers, and on school districts. Achievement data in reading and math were gathered in the spring for three successive years—1997, 1998, and 1999—for students in the third through fifth grades, respectively. The data collected were "measures of students' performance, teachers' reported behavior and opinions, and the school's policy environment in seventy-one schools" from eighteen districts in seven states (DOE, PES, 2001b). The sample was not selected to be representative of high-poverty schools, the nation as a whole, or the states and districts from which the sample was drawn.

The schools in the sample all received Title I funds; most had relatively high poverty levels. Fifty-nine of the seventy-one schools were operating schoolwide programs in 1998–1999. (The number with schoolwide programs increased from fifty-eight in 1997–1998 and from fifty-four in 1996–1997.) The sample was selected from states and districts that had previously enacted standards-based reform approaches (DOE, PES 2001b vol. 2, 4–5). The study period saw a general movement toward more schoolwide programs and more standards-based reform.

The quite different analytical approach of the LESCP study, as compared with the longitudinal Prospects Study, for example, reflected changes in the conceptual framework for the role and function of Title I (evident in the 1994 amendments that encouraged schoolwide programs). Title I policy is now oriented toward raising achievement across the board in schools to meet standards that would in principle be applicable to all schools, whatever the income levels of families whose children attended these schools. The concept differs markedly from the traditional Title I ideology of providing remedial services to a portion of children in high-poverty areas on the basis of deficiencies in their achievement.

Movement toward an approach that emphasized common standards was supported in part by Prospects Study data. Those data indicated that the actual level of achievement reached by children in high-poverty schools was much lower than the level for children in low-poverty schools to whom teachers gave comparable grades. Support for school-wide approaches was also buttressed by shortcomings evident from experience with compensatory activities that singled out individual students for special Title I services such as pullout programs. Those changes made it seem less appropriate to see Title I services as treatments applied to selected students with evaluation oriented toward measuring the effects of the treatment on performance. The focus of the evaluation accordingly shifted away from measuring the impact of participation in Title I toward assessing the impact of policies and practices implemented under the new Title I framework. The emphasis in the Longitudinal Evaluation study was identifying specific policies, approaches, and teaching practices that influenced student performance and measuring the magnitude of their impact (DOE, PES 2001b, vol. 1, 4, and vol. 22, 4).

The final report noted that "students in the LESCP schools, on average, did not catch up with national norms during the course of the study" (DOE, PSE, 2001b, vol. 1, 1). The schools in the sample, of course, were those furthest along in implementing the new conceptual and programmatic approach to Title I. Regarding specific practices associated with improved student performance in both reading and math, outreach by teachers to parents of low-achieving students was apparently the most reliable and quantitatively important contributor to improved achievement for students with low initial achievement levels (DOE, PSE, vol. 1, 18). Other features, such as teachers' rating of their own professional development, sometimes showed slight, but not always consistent, effects on student achievement. The results produced no strong or robust conclusions about the validity and promise of the new framework for Title I implementation. "The study's findings lend some support to the policy position that a framework, including standards, assessments, and professional development, can improve student achievement when teachers are engaged with that framework" (DOE, PSE, 2001b, vol. 1, 18).

Summary

The emphasis on evaluation of Title I's effectiveness resulted in many studies oriented toward measuring the impact of the program. The data analyzed and the methods used in those studies varied greatly. The studies that examined the effects of Title I on achievement differ somewhat in the emphasis of their conclusions, and the evidence that they provide is not always consistent between studies. Several significant efforts have been made to reexamine these various studies and to summarize their results. It might be an exaggeration to claim that there is a consensus about what the best evidence shows. Nonetheless there is considerable agreement about the broad picture portrayed by the studies.

Summary statements in reviews of research often consider the impact of Title I on the achievement gap. Quotations from two 1996 reviews illustrate similarities in the views of authors with different professional and research experience. A scholarly study, a meta-analysis of evaluation results, noted:

> The evidence from Title I evaluations indicated that the program has not fulfilled its original expectation: to close the achievement gap between at-risk students and their more advantaged peers. However, Title I alone cannot be expected to serve as the great equalizer. The results do suggest, however, that without the program, children served over the last 30 years would have fallen farther behind academically. (Borman and D'Agostino 1996, 324)[8]

In the second, a Congressional Research Service report, a senior specialist in education finance who has followed Title I policies closely for many years stated:

While the achievement gains of Title I participants are generally (although not always) found to be significantly (in a statistical sense) greater than projections or estimates (based on comparison groups or other methods) of what they would be without Title I services, the gains are nevertheless not adequate to raise most participants to "adequate" or "average" levels of achievement. On average, Title I participants tend to increase their achievements levels at approximately the same rate as nondisadvantaged pupils, so "gaps" in achievement do not significantly change. (Riddle 1996, 17)[9]

Both statements suggest that Title I may have a positive impact. But if so, its effects are too small to produce any noticeable effects on the achievement gap for children from low-income families.

4

A New Evaluation of Achievement
in the 1990s

Many studies have evaluated the impact of participation in Title I on achievement. The quality of such studies has gradually improved, both because better data were developed and improved statistical techniques were available to analyze the data. This chapter builds in three ways on the evidence developed in earlier studies and summarized in chapter 3. First, we examine data not previously used to evaluate the impact of Title I. Second, we examine evidence on recent performance during the 1990s so that the results can be compared with evidence from earlier studies. Third, the data that we examine span a period when the policy emphasis changed significantly: thus we can examine the possible effects of recent changes in the implementation of Title I.[1]

The data used in this analysis are the scores of individual students on National Assessment of Educational Progress (NAEP) tests, along with information on relevant personal, family, and other characteristics. Beginning in 1993–1994, the data included whether a student received Title I services. We examine the effect of Title I on NAEP test scores in reading and math for students in the fourth and eighth grades tested in the 1993–1994, 1995–1996, and 1997–1998 school years.

The 1994 reauthorization legislation, effective October of that year, instituted important changes in the implementation of Title I. Those changes were based on a new rationale for Title I educational policy and a new emphasis on raising standards and performance for all students. The new policy resulted in more widespread use of Title I funds for schoolwide programs. Although the 1994 reauthorization stimulated changes in Title I implementation, the introduction of changes consistent with the new direction of policy began before the legislation was enacted, and full implementation of the 1994 legislation was still in process in 1997–1998. Nevertheless, the changes in implementation during the 1990s were pronounced, and the data that we examined provided an opportunity to look for at least preliminary evidence that the new policies were improving the effectiveness of Title I.

The NAEP data are the only recent major national data sets with student-level information on academic performance and Title I status.[2] In addition to information on achievement and Title I, the NAEP data contain extensive information on students, households, teachers, and schools. Although the NAEP data contain much useful information for examining student achievement, the data are only cross-sectional; that is, they refer to only one period. The data do not include information on the student's achievement level before receiving Title I services or on subsequent performance. Neither remedial services nor student performance is traced over time. The cross-sectional nature of the data, of course, limits the contribution that they can make to evaluating Title I. The estimates in this study are based on cross-sectional comparisons of students receiving Title I services with otherwise similar students not receiving Title I services.

For our analysis we use state NAEP data instead of main NAEP data for two reasons.[3] First, microdata from the 1995–1996 main NAEP math assessment were not publicly available. Second, for each assessment the state NAEP sample is much larger than the main NAEP sample. The main NAEP typically samples less than 10,000 students for each grade or subject, while the state NAEP samples about 2,500 students per state for each grade or subject with at least 36 states participating in each assessment since 1993–1994. The state NAEP samples are not nationally representative because all states did not participate. The state NAEP data in this study, however, are weighted to be representative of the population of students in the states sampled.

The following section describes a model of student achievement. The third section discusses the data used to estimate the model, followed by a discussion of the model estimates in the fourth section. The fifth section summarizes results and discusses policy implications of the analysis. A final section briefly summarizes the conclusions.

The Model

Student achievement is modeled in a standard "educational production function" framework:

$$\text{Achievement} = f(\text{Title I}, ST, H, T, SC, SE). \tag{4-1}$$

Title I identifies students receiving Title I services. ST is a set of other student-level characteristics. H is a set of household characteristics. T is a set of teacher characteristics. SC is a set of school characteristics, and SE is a set of community socioeconomic characteristics.

Because students are not randomly selected to receive Title I services, estimates that do not account for the selection process may be biased. The effects of Title I on achievement are consequently estimated in a model that takes the selection process into account:

$$\text{Title I} = f(DI, SCH, STU). \tag{4-2}$$

DI is a set of district variables influencing a student's chance of receiving Title I services. SCH is a set of school characteristics influencing the student's probability of being selected as a Title I student. STU is a set of student factors affecting the probability the student receives Title I services.

The Data

The data used to examine effects of Title I on achievement include three different school years (1993–1994, 1995–1996, and 1997–1998), two different grades (fourth and eighth), and two different subjects (reading and math). Only five sets of coefficients are estimated for each specification of the model, however, because reading was tested only for the fourth grade in 1993–1994. For both fourth and eighth grades, math was tested in 1995–1996 and reading in 1997–1998. The size of the sample of individual students examined for each of the five sets of estimates ranges from 82,748 to 100,297.

Endogenous Variables. We treat two variables as endogenous: achievement and Title I participation. The achievement measures employed in this study are from the state NAEP reading and mathematics tests. Data are analyzed for public schools in all states sampled plus the District of Columbia.[4] Table 4-1 reports descriptive statistics for achievement measures by year and grade.

To take into account possible selection bias, we must also regard the Title I status of students as endogenous. A dummy variable equal to one identifies students who receive Title I services. Table 4-1 also includes descriptive statistics for the Title I student dummy showing the proportion of students receiving Title I services.

Achievement measures. Achievement as measured by NAEP test scores is not as straightforward as simply the score received by individual students. The student is not asked to answer all questions on the NAEP test. Instead matrix sampling is employed such that the questions answered by each student are a subset of all questions used in the test. To measure a student's achievement, five plausible values are generated based on the student's actual responses and those of students with the same personal characteristics and the same answers (DOE, NCES 1999). That process supposedly yields an unbiased estimate of a student's score if the student had taken the entire exam. We use the mean of each student's five plausible values from the state NAEP to measure achievement in math or reading.[5]

Title I indicator. Title I experienced important changes during the sample period of 1993–1994 to 1997–1998. Perhaps the most important change affecting participation in Title I was the shift toward school-wide programs, allowed in schools with a minimum percentage of students in poverty. The 1994 reauthorization legislation reduced the poverty threshold for eligibility for schoolwide programs from 75 percent to 60 percent in 1995–1996 and to 50 percent for subsequent years. The percentage of Title I schools operating schoolwide programs increased from 10 percent in 1994–1995 to 45 percent in 1997–1998.[6]

At least in part as a consequence of the shift toward schoolwide programs, the ways in which Title I services were provided to students

Table 4-1 Descriptive Statistics for Achievement and Title I Variables

Mean NAEP Value	Weighted Mean[a]	Standard Deviation
4th-grade reading, 1993–94	210.67	37.90
4th-grade math, 1995–96	221.26	29.85
8th-grade math, 1995–96	269.16	34.50
4th-grade reading, 1997–98	213.68	35.37
8th-grade reading, 1997–98	260.47	31.20

Student Title I Dummy	Weighted Mean[a]	Standard Deviation
4th-grade reading, 1993–94	.195	.396
4th-grade math, 1995–96	.220	.414
8th-grade math, 1995–96	.127	.333
4th-grade reading, 1997–98	.305	.461
8th-grade reading, 1997–98	.178	.383

a. Weighted by sampling weights.

also changed. The percentage of schools using pullout programs declined from 74 percent of Title I schools in 1991–1992 to 68 percent in 1997–1998. During the same period the percentage of schools providing in-class services increased from 58 to 83 percent (DOE, PES 1999, xv).

The allocation of funds also changed over the sample period. Between 1993–1994 and 1997–1998 Title I expenditures increased from $6.9 billion to $8 billion (a 7 percent real increase). By some measures Title I funds have also become more targeted toward poor schools. In 1993–1994 79 percent of the highest-poverty schools (those with 75–100 percent of students eligible for subsidized lunches) received Title I funds. By 1997–1998 95 percent of the highest-poverty schools received Title I funds (DOE, PES 2001a). The proportion of public schools receiving Title I funds declined from 62 percent in 1993–1994 to 58 percent in 1997–1998 (DOE, PES 1999).

Although the shift of Title I resources toward poorer schools might increase resources for poor students, the shift toward schoolwide programs could have the opposite effect. Table 4-2 reports characteristics of

Table 4-2 Selected Characteristics of Title I Students

Weighted Means	4th Grade				8th Grade		
	1993–94	1995–96	1997–98	% Change 1994–98	1995–96	1997–98	% Change 1996–98
LEP student	0.10	0.11	0.08	–15.4	0.08	0.11	46.8
White student	0.38	0.36	0.40	4.1	0.27	0.27	2.0
Black student	0.28	0.28	0.27	–0.9	0.28	0.28	–0.6
Hispanic student	0.28	0.30	0.27	–4.0	0.38	0.38	0.7
Native-American student	0.03	0.03	0.03	–8.5	0.02	0.03	10.2
Asian student	0.03	0.03	0.04	2.0	0.05	0.04	–18.6
Female student	0.49	0.49	0.50	2.8	0.50	0.50	0.8
Subsidized lunch student	0.65	0.71	0.69	6.7	0.71	0.70	–2.2
School % subsidized lunch	61.30	69.86	68.40	11.6	63.93	68.85	7.7
School % Title I	N/A	58.99	74.40	N/A	60.95	74.91	22.9
Urban area	0.38	0.44	0.44	14.5	0.46	0.46	–0.2
Rural area	0.20	0.16	0.16	–21.5	0.15	0.14	–1.5
District child poverty rate	25.37	28.47	24.68	–2.7	31.49	28.12	–10.7
Real median household income	33,543.55	33,805.95	34,929.69	4.1	32,875.91	33,224.71	1.1
Northeast	0.18	0.19	0.11	–38.1	0.13	0.11	–10.5

Southeast and West rows (continuation of preceding table):

	1993–94	1995–96	1997–98	% Change 1994–98	1995–96	1997–98	% Change 1996–98
Southeast	0.32	0.31	0.33	4.5	0.28	0.29	3.6
West	0.38	0.39	0.43	13.7	0.50	0.52	5.2

Weighted Percentage of Students Receiving Title I for Selected Groups

	4th Grade			% Change	8th Grade		% Change
	1993–94	1995–96	1997–98	1994–98	1995–96	1997–98	1996–98
All students	19.5	22.0	30.5	56.4	12.7	17.8	40.2
White students	11.8	12.6	20.0	69.5	5.4	8.1	50.0
Black students	35.7	41.0	52.1	45.9	23.7	31.9	34.6
Hispanic students	33.7	39.2	48.2	43.0	30.3	38.4	26.7
Native American students	27.5	27.9	37.3	35.6	17.7	26.3	48.6
Asians students	16.8	19.7	24.4	45.2	14.1	14.8	5.0
Subsidized lunch students	29.9	39.3	49.9	66.9	27.2	35.2	29.4
Nonsubsidized lunch students	12.1	10.6	16.5	36.4	5.8	8.6	48.3
Number of States and Schools							
States	41	43 + D.C.	40 + D.C.		40 + D.C.	36 + D.C.	
Schools	4,076	4,406	4,038		3,668	3,274	
Title I Schools	3,008	2,722	2,662		1,411	1,370	

NOTE: Weighted by sampling weights.

Title I students in our analysis (the number of states and schools sampled are also reported). Those data show that the percentage of students receiving Title I, consistent with increased use of schoolwide programs, has increased significantly during the sample period. The percentage of fourth graders in the state NAEP receiving Title I services increased from 19.5 percent in 1993–1994 to 30.5 percent in 1997–1998. Similarly the percentage of eighth graders receiving Title I funds increased from 12.7 in 1995–1996 to 17.8 in 1997–1998.

Other data from our samples provide rather inconclusive information about targeting. The percentage of fourth-grade Title I students receiving subsidized lunches increased from 65 in 1993–1994 to 69 in 1997–1998, but the percentage of eighth graders in those circumstances decreased slightly. While the percentage of the sample's fourth-grade students who were black or Hispanic increased from 31 to 33 percent, the percentage of all students receiving Title I services who were members of those minorities declined slightly. The racial breakdown of eighth-grade Title I students changed little during the sample period. On the whole, little evidence from state NAEP summary statistics indicates that Title I resources have been significantly shifted toward poorer students in recent years.[7]

Major differences in Title I services across grades emerged. In 1997–1998 about two-thirds of elementary schools received Title I funds, compared with only 29 percent of secondary schools. In 1996–1997 Title I services reached 30 percent of students in grades four through six, 15 percent of students in grades seven through nine, and 5 percent of students in grades ten through twelve (DOE, PES 1999). Funding per student also differs by grade. In 1997–1998 Title I funding per poor student was $495 in elementary schools and $372 in secondary schools (DOE, PES 2001a). For the sample of Title I students in this study, Hispanics (whites) are a larger (smaller) percentage of eighth graders than fourth graders. Eighth-grade Title I students may have received Title I or other compensatory educational services longer than fourth graders. Because of differences across time and grades in Title I services and students, separate estimates are reported for each year and grade.

State NAEP sample information on Title I on the percentage of students receiving Title I services closely agrees with national estimates reported in other sources. State NAEP data about the student-level and school-level Title I variables also generally agree. For the eighth-grade sample in 1995–1996, 9 percent of students sampled received Title I services, as did 10 percent of all eighth graders. But information provided by school administrators for the state NAEP data apparently show some errors. The eighth-grade sample in 1997–1998, for instance, has 114 students coded as receiving Title I services in twenty-nine schools that are not coded as being Title I eligible. In the 121 schools in the 1995–1996 fourth-grade sample with 100 percent of students reported as receiving Title I services, some students are not coded as Title I students. Unfortunately the Department of Education's Public Elementary/ Secondary School Universe Data provide no school-level information on Title I until school year 1998–1999. Therefore the Title I status of schools in this study is not readily verifiable. The sample selection model (discussed below) can, however, help alleviate bias due to Title I reporting error.

Achievement Equation Exogenous Variables

Student-level characteristics include binary indicators for individual education plan (IEP) students,[8] limited English proficiency (LEP) students, black, Hispanic, Native-American, and Asian students; females; and students completing an hour or more of homework per night. For 1993–1994, ST uses a single-dummy variable for students receiving free or reduced price lunches. For 1995–1996 and 1997–1998, ST contains separate dummy variables for reduced price and free lunch students. ST also includes continuous variables for student age and hours of TV viewing per day.[9] Because Title I funds might affect time spent on homework or TV, some of our estimates exclude those variables (along with the teacher variables discussed below). Table 4-3 reports weighted means by grade for all exogenous variables in the achievement equation.

For all years, household characteristics in H include dummies for households with fathers who are high school graduates (but not college graduates), fathers who are college graduates, mothers who are high

Table 4-3 Descriptive Statistics for Achievement Equation Exogenous Variables

	4th Grade		8th Grade	
	Weighted mean	% imputed	Weighted mean	% imputed
Student age	9.97	0.33	14.03	0.58
IEP student	0.06	0.00	0.06	0.00
LEP student	0.04	0.00	0.03	0.00
Black	0.15	0.18	0.15	0.18
Hispanic	0.17	0.18	0.17	0.18
Native American	0.02	0.18	0.02	0.18
Asian	0.04	0.18	0.04	0.18
Female	0.50	0.00	0.50	0.00
Subsidized lunch	0.41	19.70	N/A	N/A
Free lunch	0.34	4.76	0.27	7.17
Reduced-price lunch	0.07	4.76	0.06	7.17
Hour or more of homework	0.45	1.99	0.62	0.74
TV per day	3.16	1.98	3.21	0.62
Reading materials	2.67	3.10	3.04	0.82
Dad HS graduate	0.34	42.89	0.45	23.30
Dad college graduate	0.40	47.17	0.32	23.30
Mom HS graduate	0.34	38.53	0.50	15.21
Mom college graduate	0.39	42.89	0.30	15.21
Dad works	0.82	5.65	0.86	19.22
Mom works	0.72	5.62	0.59	11.93
Single parent	0.24	3.08	0.25	2.45
Class size	22.53	16.74	24.18	27.73
Years teaching	13.85	5.14	13.46	7.86
Graduate degree	0.43	5.45	0.45	8.16
School % black	15.92	1.14	16.01	1.72
School % Hispanic	11.81	1.14	12.86	1.72
School % lunch program	43.64	7.57	39.69	11.86
Large city	0.16	0.00	0.15	0.00
Midsize city	0.18	0.00	0.18	0.00
Suburb, large city	0.25	0.00	0.24	0.00
Suburb, mid city	0.15	0.00	0.13	0.00
Large town	0.02	0.00	0.02	0.00
Small town	0.11	0.00	0.13	0.00
District child poverty	18.51	N/A	18.62	N/A
Median household income	$38,056.57	N/A	$38,123.71	N/A
% county age, 0–19	0.29	N/A	0.29	N/A
% county age, 20–34	0.22	N/A	0.22	N/A
% county age, 60+	0.16	N/A	0.16	N/A

school graduates (but not college graduates), and mothers who are college graduates. For 1993–1994 and 1995–1996, H includes a dummy variable for single-parent households. For 1995–1996, H includes dummies for fathers who work for pay and for mothers who work for pay. H also includes a variable for the number of reading articles (of four possible) in the home.

Teacher characteristics in T include continuous variables for class size and years taught and a dummy variable for teachers with graduate degrees. Because Title I funds might be used to reduce class size or hire more educated or experienced teachers, we also estimate equations while excluding T (along with the homework and TV measures).

School characteristics in SC include the percentage of students who are black, the percentage of students who are Hispanic, the percentage of students who receive subsidized lunches, and six urbanistic dummies (for large cities, mid-size cities, suburbs of large cities, suburbs of mid-size cities, large towns, and small towns; rural areas are relegated to the intercept).

SE socioeconomic data include the school district poverty rate for children ages five to seventeen, county real median household income, the percentage of the county aged zero to nineteen, the percentage of the county aged twenty to thirty-four, the percentage of the county aged sixty and older,[10] and regional or state dummies.[11] All variables in SE were matched to the autumn of the school year (that is, school district poverty rates for 1995 were matched to NAEP data for school year 1995–1996). We deleted observations with missing SE variables from the sample.

Data Sources and Description. All student, household, teacher, and school information was extracted from NAEP data. Although data on Title I status included all students, some other NAEP information was missing for a significant number of students. For fourth-graders in 1995–1996, for example, data on father's education were missing for half the students, and data on class size were missing for 40 percent of the students. Dropping observations with any missing variables would decrease the sample size drastically for all samples. For instance, dropping cases with missing NAEP variables would reduce the sample of fourth graders in 1993–1994 from 94,966 students to 31,401 students. There-fore missing cases for the exogenous NAEP variables were imputed.[12] Table 4-3 indicates the percentage of cases imputed for those variables. Imputed data were constrained to the range of observed data, and the process had virtually no impact on means or standard deviations.

In addition to problems with missing data, reporting error is a potentially significant issue for some NAEP exogenous variables. Grissmer and colleagues (2000) compared NAEP student-reported data with census data for similar families. They found that student-reported racial-ethnic data closely agreed with census data. But they noted that NAEP student-reported data on parental education tended to be overstated relative to census data. Fourth graders in our study reported higher levels of parental education relative to eighth graders: 48 percent of fourth graders reported both mothers and fathers with college degrees. Of eighth graders in our sample, 34 percent reported fathers and mothers with college degrees, and 32 percent reported mothers having graduated college. In March 1998, 31.8 percent of the population aged twenty-five and older had college degrees according to census data (DOE, NCES 2000a). The reporting error for parental education is probably more serious for fourth graders than for eighth graders in this study. The percentage of parental education data missing is also much greater for fourth graders than for eighth graders.

Age is also misreported for at least some students. For fourth graders in 1998, for instance, reported student ages ranged from minus twenty to seventy-seven. For this study, student age was imputed for students with reported ages more than two years (about two standard deviations) from the mean. To assess the importance of problems of missing data and report- ing error, we estimated equations without measures of parental education and labor force status, as well as without observations with missing data. Limiting the model and sample in that way had little impact on our estimates; thus those estimates are not reported. School district poverty rates for 1993 were interpolated, and in some cases county poverty rates replaced missing data. The National Center for Education Statistics (NCES) provided data on school district poverty for

1990; the Census Bureau provided data for 1995 and 1997. All county data came from the Census Bureau.

Title I Equation Exogenous Variables

Obtaining reliable estimates requires variables in the Title I equation that (1) significantly influence a student's chance of receiving Title I services and (2) have no independent effect on achievement. We use district- and school-level variables based on the Title I allocation formula, which we believe reasonably satisfy both criteria. The Title I allocation process and our choice of variables for the Title I equation are discussed next.

School district Title I allocations. The federal government bases Title I allocations to school districts on a "complex formula that incorporates, among other factors, the average per-pupil expenditure in the state, the number of children in poverty, and previous allocations to the state and to the district" (GAO 2000, 26). Title I funds are bypass aid that flows to districts through states. States, however, have only limited discretion in making final allocations to districts.

Although child poverty counts primarily determine district allocations, numerous factors result in substantial variation across districts in Title I funding per poor child. Hold-harmless provisions, for example, limit decreases in district allocations when poverty counts change. Special minimum provisions for small states also create variation in Title I funding per poor student. The federal formula includes average state per pupil expenditure to adjust for differences across states in the cost of education. As a practical result, districts in states with relatively high spending on education receive greater Title I funding.[13] In addition the poverty counts determining allocations lag by varying years. Data from the 1990 census were first used in the federal Title I formula in 1993–1994. Changes in child poverty counts between the 1980 and 1990 census caused abrupt changes in district allocations starting in 1993–1994, subject to hold-harmless provisions (Gordon 2001). States can also choose their own poverty measures in making final district allocations, which can result in further variation in Title I funding per pupil.

School district exogenous variables. To control for district factors influencing the probability of student selection for Title I services, *DI* includes district Title I expenditures per pupil. As noted above, exogenous political economy factors such as hold-harmless provisions result in variation among otherwise similar school districts in Title I funding per student. A student's chances of receiving Title I funding should be positively related to district Title I spending per student. Thus random differences in Title I funding per student across districts cause variation in a student's chances of receiving Title I services that is unrelated to student achievement. *DI* also includes the school district poverty rate and the district percentages of subsidized lunch, black, and Hispanic students as proxies for the portion of students in the district eligible for Title I.[14]

School Title I allocations. School districts are required to allocate Title I funds to schools based on numbers of low-income students, usually measured by subsidized lunch students (GAO 2000; DOE, PES 1999). "A school is eligible if its school attendance area has a poverty rate that is at least equal to the district average poverty rate or 35 percent (whichever is less)" (DOE, PES 1999, 74).

School exogenous variables. School variables influencing the student's chances of receiving Title I funding include three based on the percentage of students in the school receiving subsidized lunches. The first variable is the school percentage of subsidized lunch students in schools where the percentage is (1) less than 35 percent *and* (2) less than the district average (thus making the school ineligible for Title I). The second variable is the school percentage of subsidized lunch students in schools where the percentage is (1) greater than or equal to 35 percent *or* (2) greater than or equal to the district average (thus making the school eligible for Title I). The third variable is a dummy for schools with subsidized lunch participation rates at or above the threshold for schoolwide Title I programs.

The identification strategy assumes that controlling for the percentage of students receiving subsidized lunches (and other variables in *SC*), the percentage above or below certain formula amounts is exogenous. Because school districts are not required to allocate Title I funds based on subsidized lunch participation, school percentages of black and Hispanic students are included in *SCH* as proxies for other possible poverty measures used to allocate Title I funds. *SCH* includes urbanicity and state dummies to capture unmeasured differences in Title I allocations. School-level demographic data were extracted from the NAEP data.

Student Title I eligibility. Within schools academic need regardless of economic circumstances supposedly determines a student's Title I eligibility. The extent to which former criteria still influence inclusion for schoolwide programs, however, is not clear. Although low achievement may determine Title I participation within schools, participation is not based on NAEP scores because those scores are not published for individual students (or schools or districts). NAEP scores and other standardized test scores can also be substantially different. In their study for RAND, for example, Klein and his colleagues (2000) found significant differences between scores on the Texas Assessment of Academic Skills with Texas NAEP scores.

Student exogenous variables. Because no information on prior academic performance is available, student factors affecting the probability of selection for Title I services are controlled for in the reduced form. Exogenous student factors measuring a student's chances of receiving Title I services include the student's age, subsidized lunch status, gender, race and ethnic background, IEP and LEP status, measures of parental education, a measure of parental labor market status (for 1995–1996), single-parent household status (for 1993–1994 and 1995–1996), and number of reading materials in the home.

Estimates

For estimates of the effects of Title I services on achievement, we used a "treatment effects" model that corrects for selection bias that can result from systematic unmeasured differences between Title I and non–Title I students. The treatment effects estimator is a sample selection model that uses data on characteristics and performance of both students who receive Title I services and those who do not. The model produces estimates of the components of achievement measures attributable to differences in characteristics of the students in the two groups and differences that are attributable to participation in Title I.[15]

Treatment effect equations were estimated by a maximum likelihood method. Observations for all regressions were weighted to be representative of the student population in the states sampled.[16] Robust standard errors were computed by adjustments needed to correct for the sample design.[17] The appendix contains estimates from the probit equations for selection of students into Title I.

Both reasoning and statistical evidence support the appropriateness of treating the explanatory variable in the achievement equation as endogenous and of using a treatment effects model to deal with selection bias. At least within schools students are supposedly selected into Title I based on academic need. As discussed above, however, the NAEP data lack information on past student performance. The exogenous variables in the achievement equation control to some extent for past student performance. But unmeasured differences likely remain between Title I and non–Title I students in our sample.

The Wald test statistics confirm the importance of latent differences between Title I and non–Title I students for most equations reported in the tables that follow. Most of those equations show negative and significant correlations between the residuals of the Title I and achievement equations. The correlations indicate systematic unmeasured differences between Title I students and non–Title I students that are associated with (1) increased likelihood of receiving Title I and (2) lower NAEP scores. Consequently estimates treating the Title I variable as exogenous are likely to be biased because of unmeasured factors related to both Title I participation and achievement. After some initial comparisons with least squares estimates, all estimates discussed subsequently come from treatment effects models with the same basic structure. To examine the sensitivity of results to different approaches, we report and discuss estimates from various specifications. Table 4-4 summarizes the alternatives reported and discussed.

Table 4-4 Summary of Alternative Specifications and Samples

Table	Panel	Sample	Linear	Nonlinear (Box-Cox)	All Variables	Limited Variables	Regional Dummies	State Fixed Effect
4-5	Top	Full	✓					✓
4-5	Bottom	Full		✓				✓
4-6	Top	Full	✓					✓
4-6	Bottom	Full		✓				✓
4-7	Top	Full	✓		✓		✓	
4-7	Bottom	Full		✓	✓		✓	
4-8	Top	Full	✓		✓	✓	✓	
4-8	Bottom	Full		✓	✓	✓	✓	
4-9	Top	White	✓			✓		✓
4-9	Bottom	Minority	✓			✓		✓
4-10	Top	White		✓		✓		✓
4-10	Bottom	Minority		✓		✓		✓
4-11	Top	Nonsubsidized lunch	✓			✓		✓
4-11	Bottom	Subsidized lunch	✓			✓		✓
4-12	Top	Nonsubsidized lunch		✓		✓		✓
4-12	Bottom	Subsidized lunch		✓		✓		✓

Estimates from both linear and nonlinear specifications of student NAEP scores are reported for all samples and other alternative specifications. Although theory provides no basis for preferring one functional form or another, linear specification is the simplest and most straightforward approach. Departures from normal distributions for achievement measures were examined with Box-Cox tests for regressions with only the exogenous variables. Box-Cox tests for functional form showed that in most cases the linear specification was rejected in favor of a power transformation of the dependent variable.[18] Separate tests were performed for each grade and year. Tests were also performed for student subgroups within each grade and year (the results are discussed below). The estimated Box-Cox parameters used to transform student NAEP scores are reported for each nonlinear equation. The case for estimating equations after transforming the dependent variable by using the appropriate estimated Box-Cox parameter is purely empirical.

Another issue concerns whether regressions should be estimated with regional or state fixed-effects. The influence of policies at the state level for elementary and secondary education suggests the merit of using state dummies to capture variation specific to states. If a component of differences in achievement among states is attributable to Title I, however, using regional dummy variables to take into account differences in costs, prices, or other characteristics common to neighboring states may be preferable.

Still another issue is the appropriateness of regarding all variables in the achievement equation listed in table 4-3 as exogenous. Title I funds could have been used to hire better-qualified teachers, or Title I participation could affect student characteristics such as time spent on homework or watching TV. To take such possibilities into account, we estimated equations by using a limited variable set, excluding measures of class size, teacher education and experience, homework, and TV viewing.

In addition to the estimates for the five full samples reported for each specification, we also report estimates for subsamples chosen because of their particular relevance to the goals of Title I. A subsample of children from relatively poor families was chosen on the basis of participation in a subsidized lunch program, and a subsample of minority children identified as black, Hispanic, or Native American. Because one of the goals of Title I is raising the performance of poor and minority students and because effects might be different for them than for others, we examine the evidence for students in these subsamples. Box-Cox tests were also performed for each subsample. In general, NAEP score distributions for minority and subsidized lunch students tend to be closer to normal than distributions for more advantaged students. As a result, estimates for minority and subsidized lunch students should be less sensitive to functional form than estimates for whites and nonsubsidized lunch students.

Estimates for All Students in Full Samples

To begin the discussion of empirical results, consider the treatment effects estimates of the Title I effect correcting for selectivity reported in table 4-5. That table and subsequent tables report only the Title I coefficients. The appendix reports coefficients for the full set of explanatory variables for equations in table 4-5. The table reports estimates of the Title I effect for all five samples for both linear and nonlinear specifications. Table 4-5 also reports Wald test statistics for total significance of the achievement equations and correlations between the error terms of the achievement and Title I equations. The table also shows estimates of rho (the correlation of the error terms between the achievement and Title I equations), the Title I effect (measured in standard deviations), the expected difference in NAEP scores between Title I and other students, the expected difference between Title I students and other students absent Title I, and the percentage change in the absolute value of the Title I and non–Title I gap due to Title I. In addition to treatment effects estimates, the table reports weighted least squares estimates for the linear specification to illustrate the importance of selection bias.

The least squares estimate of the Title I effect for fourth-grade reading in 1993–1994 is –25.12. The estimated effect after taking into account selection bias—the treatment effect estimate—in the top panel of table 4-5 is –14.23. The estimated total differential for Title I students is of

Table 4-5 Effects of Title I on Achievement with Estimates for Full Sample with All Variables and State Fixed Effects

Linear Equation Estimates	1993–94 Reading	1995–96 Math		1997–98 Reading	
	4th grade	4th grade	8th grade	4th grade	8th grade
Title I estimate (t-value)	−14.23*** (9.14)	−3.79** (2.29)	2.70 (1.20)	−2.77* (1.68)	1.63 (1.25)
N	94,966	100,297	86,908	96,564	82,742
Wald test chi²(d.f.)[a]	13,186.70*** (75)	14,604.06*** (81)	171,183.4*** (78)	9,787.76*** (71)	13,838.73*** (71)
Rho (standard error)	−0.22 (0.02)	−0.29 (0.03)	−0.29 (0.04)	−0.16 (0.03)	−0.16 (0.03)
Wald test chi²(1)[b]	79.10***	60.93***	42.75***	26.29***	30.85***
Effect in standard deviations	−0.38	−0.13	0.08	−0.08	0.05
Title I differential	−26.49	−16.56	−14.35	−11.03	−6.87
No treatment differential	−12.26	−12.77	−17.04	−8.26	−8.50
% change in achievement gap	118.50	30.34	−16.66	34.40	−20.32
WLS estimate[c] (t-stat)	−25.12*** (37.37)	−14.95*** (24.96)	−9.70*** (11.59)	−9.78*** (12.04)	−4.44*** (6.04)

Nonlinear Estimates[d]	1993–94 Reading		1995–96 Math			1997–98 Reading		
	4th grade		4th grade		8th grade		4th grade		8th grade
Title I estimate (t-value)	−1.06	(0.69)	−.56	(0.33)	4.10*	(1.76)	2.51	(1.37)	6.05***	(3.84)
N	94,966		100,297		86,908		96,564		82,742
Box-Cox parameter	1.63		1.27		1.12		1.80		2.06
Wald test chi2(d.f.)[a]	13,670.55***	(75)	14,467.56***	(81)	17,231.18***	(78)	10,696.99***	(75)	15,270.84***	(71)
Rho (standard error)	−.46	(.02)	−.36	(.04)	−.32	(.04)	−.27	(.04)	−.28	(.04)
Wald test chi2(1)[b]	277.13***		139.89***		46.81***		53.64***		46.92***
Effect in standard deviations	−0.06		−0.02		0.12		0.07		0.19
Title I differential	−27.74		−16.89		−14.81		−11.57		−8.29
No treatment differential	−26.68		−16.33		−18.91		−14.08		−14.34
% change in achievement gap	4.03		−3.48		−22.80		−18.24		−44.37

*10% significance level. **5% significance level. ***1% significance level. (t-tests are two-tailed tests.)

NOTE: Coefficients of the exogenous variables in the linear equation are reported in the appendix. Exogenous coefficients for the nonlinear equation are not reported.

a. Test for overall significance of achievement equations.

b. Test for independence of achievement and Title I equations.

c. WLS estimates are weighted least-squares coefficients for Title I participation.

d. Estimates with Box-Cox transformations of achievement measures. Treatment effect estimates are scaled for conformity with untransformed achievement measures.

approximately the same magnitude as the least squares estimate (–.26.49 compared with –25.12). Absent Title I services, the estimates indicate that Title I students would be expected to score 12.26 points below other students, given their characteristics. Title I services widen the estimated gap between Title I and non–Title students by an additional 14.23 points. The weighted least squares coefficients for the other four samples are considerably smaller than for the 1993–1994 reading sample, but all are negative and significant. In contrast, two treatment effect coefficients for those linear equations are positive, though not statistically significant, and illustrate the difference that taking selection bias into account can make.

Consider next the treatment effect estimates reported in the bottom panel of table 4-5 that result from the power transformation of the dependent variable based on Box-Cox procedures. Although three of the five treatment effect estimates are positive for the nonlinear equation, only one is statistically significant at the conventional 5 percent level. The results for fourth-grade reading in 1993–1994 show the most striking difference between the two equations, where the large (–.38 standard deviation) and statistically significant negative coefficient becomes small (–.06 standard deviation) and not statistically significant. The estimated effects for the other samples are generally small (less than .2 standard deviations) and in most instances not statistically significant.

The estimates reported in table 4-6 differ from those in table 4-5 by the exclusion of some variables that might be affected by Title I, specifically teacher characteristics, class size, student homework habits, and TV viewing. These estimates from equations with limited variable sets show much the same pattern as in table 4-5. All of the estimates in table 4-6 are more positive (either smaller in absolute value if negative or larger in absolute value if positive) than those in table 4-5. Those results might be expected if the limited variable sets leave more scope for Title I effects. Yet the differences are quite small relative to the estimated coefficients. Indeed most estimates of Title I effects in both tables are not statistically significant, and the significant estimated Title I effects are as likely to be negative as positive.

The estimates reported in tables 4-7 and 4-8 result from equations that parallel those in tables 4-5 and 4-6 with the substitution of regional fixed-effects (regional dummy variables) for state fixed-effects. A comparison of tables 4-7 and 4-8 shows more similarities than differences. In particular the pattern of statistically significant coefficients is similar in the two tables. The most prevalent results are quantitatively small and statistically insignificant coefficients. In all four tables the Box-Cox transformation eliminates the large, significant, negative coefficient for fourth-grade reading in 1993–1994 and results in statistically insignificant coefficient estimates.

A comparison of tables 4-7 and 4-8 with their counterparts (tables 4-5 and 4-6) tells much the same story. In some instances there are differences in signs as well as statistical significance of coefficients, but no instances occur with sign changes when both coefficients are statistically significant. Those estimates from full samples, taken together, do not provide any persuasive evidence of systematic positive effects of Title I participation. And although differences in specifications lead to some noticeable differences in patterns of coefficients, many differences across specifications are not large, and there seems to be little basis for choosing one as preferable to another.

Estimates for Subsamples

Tables 4-9 and 4-10 report comparisons of the estimated effects of Title I for minority and white students. Estimates from linear equations reported in table 4-9 again show that the predominant patterns for both white and minority students are small and insignificant effects. Compared with estimates from earlier tables, the large and negative coefficients common for linear coefficients for fourth-grade reading in 1993–1994 in full sample estimates are also evident for white students, but not for minorities. The estimated Title I effect for minorities is positive and statistically significant for one sample, eighth-grade reading in 1995–1996. Again, as with linear estimates for the full sample and for white students, the Box-Cox transformation reduces to insignificance the large, negative, and statistically significant estimate for fourth-grade reading in 1993–1994. Positive and significant coefficients are estimated

Table 4-6 Effects of Title I on Achievement with Estimates for Full Sample with Limited Variable List and State Fixed Effects

Linear Equation Estimates	1993–94 Reading	1995–96 Math		1997–98 Reading	
	4th grade	4th grade	8th grade	4th grade	8th grade
Title I estimate (t-value)	−13.59*** (8.69)	−3.49** (2.11)	3.59 (1.53)	−2.50* (1.48)	2.04 (1.57)
N	94,966	100,297	86,908	96,564	82,742
Wald test chi²(d.f.)[a]	12,645.91*** (70)	14,169.46*** (76)	16,409.08*** (73)	9,165.70*** (70)	12,136.16*** (66)
Rho (standard error)	−0.24 (0.02)	−0.30 (0.03)	−0.31 (0.04)	−0.16 (0.03)	−0.17 (0.03)
Wald test chi²(1)[b]	88.71***	63.39***	46.16***	27.82***	38.51***
Effect in standard deviations	−0.36	−0.12	0.10	−0.07	0.07
Title I differential	−26.76	−16.65	−15.14	−11.20	−7.31
No treatment differential	−13.17	−13.15	−18.73	−8.70	−9.35
% change in achievement gap	105.33	27.16	−20.19	29.45	−23.08

Nonlinear Estimates[c]	1993–94 Reading		1995–96 Math			1997–98 Reading			
	4th grade		4th grade		8th grade		4th grade		8th grade
Title I estimate (t-value)[a]	0.10	(0.07)	−0.17	(0.10)	5.11*	(2.10)	3.00	(1.60)	6.71***	(4.38)
N	94,966		100,297		86,908		96,564		82,742	
Box-Cox Parameter	1.63		1.27		1.12		1.80		2.06	
Wald test chi^2(d.f.)[a]	12,986.43***	(75)	14,012.57***	(76)	16,426.21***	(73)	10,123.98***	(70)	13,301.91***	(66)
Rho (standard error)	−0.48	(0.02)	−0.37	(0.04)	−0.34	(0.04)	−0.28	(0.04)	−0.29	(0.04)
Wald test chi^2(1)[b]	321.54***		90.92***		50.83***		56.45***		58.12***	
Effect in standard deviations	0.003		−0.006		0.15		0.08		0.21	
Title I differential	−28.07		−17.00		−15.64		−11.77		−8.83	
No treatment differential	−28.17		−16.83		−20.76		−14.77		−15.54	
% change in achievement gap	−0.35		1.03		−25.91		−20.74		−45.43	

*10% significance level. **5% significance level. ***1% significance level. (t-tests are two-tailed tests.)

NOTE: Exogenous coefficients are not reported.

a. Test for overall significance of achievement equations.

b. Test for independence of achievement and Title I equations.

c. Estimates with Box-Cox transformations of achievement measures. Treatment effect estimates are scaled for conformity with untransformed achievement measures.

Table 4-7 **Effects of Title I on Achievement with Estimates for Full Samples with All Variables and Regional Fixed Effects**

Linear Equation Estimates	1993–94 Reading	1995–96 Math		1997–98 Reading	
	4th grade	4th grade	8th grade	4th grade	8th grade
Title I estimate (t-value)	−11.98*** (4.66)	0.46** (0.15)	1.02 (0.28)	3.58 (1.40)	4.06** (2.03)
N	94,966	100,297	86,908	96,564	82,742
Wald test chi^2(d.f.)[a]	11,043.35*** (38)	10,3775.05*** (41)	13,895.95*** (41)	7,888.77*** (38)	10,945.05*** (38)
Rho (standard error)	−0.27 (0.04)	−0.38 (0.06)	−0.26 (0.07)	−0.28 (0.05)	−0.21 (0.04)
Wald test chi^2(1)[b]	35.90***	92.99***	13.33***	33.81***	23.54***
Effect in standard deviations	−0.32	0.02	0.03	0.10	0.13
Title I differential	−27.19	−17.30	−14.47	−11.52	−5.77
No treatment differential	−15.20	−17.76	−15.49	−15.10	−9.83
% change in achievement gap	78.89	−0.03	−6.90	−23.71	−41.28

	1993–94 Reading		1995–96 Math			1997–98 Reading			
Nonlinear Estimates[c]	4th grade		4th grade		8th grade		4th grade		8th grade
Title I Estimate (t-value)[a]	1.15	(0.53)	3.81	(1.41)	2.35	(0.63)	8.29***	(3.45)	8.11***	(4.06)
N	94,966		100,297		86,908		96,564		82,742
Box-Cox parameter	1.63		1.27		1.12		1.80		2.06
Wald test chi^2(d.f.)[a]	11,429.89***	(38)	10,275.46***	(41)	13,951.04***	(41)	8,641.79***	(38)	12,590.48***	(38)
Rho (standard error)[b]	−0.51	(0.03)	−0.46	(0.05)	−0.29	(0.07)	−0.38	(0.04)	−0.33	(0.05)
Wald test chi^2(1)[b]	161.83***		55.58***		14.94***		64.85***		45.06***
Effect in standard deviations	0.03		0.13		0.07		0.24		0.26
Title I differential	−28.57		−17.69		−14.95		−12.17		−8.99
No treatment differential	−29.73		−21.50		−17.30		−20.47		−17.11
% change in achievement gap	−3.97		−18.08		−14.29		−41.39		−49.93

*10% significance level. **5% significance level. ***1% significance level. (t-tests are two-tailed tests.)

NOTE: Exogenous coefficients are not reported.

a. Test for overall significance of achievement equations.

b. Test for independence of achievement and Title I equations.

c. Estimates with Box-Cox transformations of achievement measures. Treatment effect estimates are scaled for conformity with untransformed achievement measures.

Table 4-8 Effects of Title I on Achievement with Estimates for Full Sample with Limited Variable List and Regional Fixed Effects

Linear Equation Estimates	1993–94 Reading	1995–96 Math		1997–98 Reading	
	4th grade	4th grade	8th grade	4th grade	8th grade
Title I estimate (t-value)	-10.33*** (3.72)	1.99 (0.67)	1.95 (0.56)	4.51* (1.73)	3.83** (2.31)
N	94,966	100,297	86,908	96,564	82,742
Wald test chi^2(d.f.)[a]	10,296.85*** (33)	9,800.21*** (36)	13,301.73*** (36)	7,310.32*** (33)	10,121.43*** (33)
Rho (standard error)	-0.30 (0.05)	-0.42 (0.06)	-0.28 (0.06)	-0.30 (0.05)	-0.21 (0.03)
Wald test chi^2(1)[b]	37.48***	38.95***	17.20***	37.18***	36.91***
Effect in standard deviations	-0.27	0.07	0.06	0.13	0.12
Title I differential	-27.27	-17.45	-15.18	-11.75	-7.73
No treatment differential	-16.94	-19.44	-17.14	-16.26	-11.56
% change in achievement gap	62.25	-10.45	-12.00	-28.47	-35.11

Nonlinear Estimates[c]	1993–94 Reading	1995–96 Math		1997–98 Reading	
	4th grade	4th grade	8th grade	4th grade	8th grade
Title I estimate (t-value)[a]	3.26 (1.54)	5.28** (2.06)	3.41 (0.95)	9.33*** (3.88)	8.27*** (4.51)
N	94,966	100,297	86,908	96,564	82,742
Box-Cox parameter	1.63	1.27	1.12	1.80	2.06
Wald test chi^2(d.f.)[a]	10,647.74*** (33)	9,684.58*** (33)	13,335.40*** (36)	7,951.87*** (33)	11,208.97*** (33)
Rho (standard error)	−0.54 (0.03)	−0.49 (0.05)	−0.31 (0.07)	−0.40 (0.04)	−0.33 (0.04)
Wald test chi^2(1)[b]	199.33***	71.44***	19.39***	73.23***	56.10***
Effect in standard deviations	0.09	0.18	0.10	0.26	0.27
Title I differential	−28.74	−17.84	−15.71	−12.44	−9.37
No treatment differential	−32.00	−23.12	−19.12	−21.77	−17.64
% change in achievement gap	−10.35	23.31	−18.75	−43.78	−49.38

*10% significance level. **5% significance level. ***1% significance level. (t-tests are two-tailed tests.)

NOTE: Exogenous coefficients are not reported.

a. Test for overall significance of achievement equations.

b. Test for independence of achievement and Title I equations.

c. Estimates with Box-Cox transformations of achievement measures. Treatment effect estimates are scaled for conformity with untransformed achievement measures.

73

Table 4-9 Effects of Title I on Achievement with Linear Estimates for White and Minority Subsamples with Limited Variable List and State Fixed Effects

White Students Linear Equation Estimates	1993–94 Reading	1995–96 Math		1997–98 Reading	
	4th grade	4th grade	8th grade	4th grade	8th grade
Title I estimate (t-value)	-20.28*** (13.22)	-5.26*** (3.06)	-1.96 (0.75)	-2.06 (1.39)	1.51 (1.02)
N	64,155	66,172	58,556	62,674	54,459
Wald test chi²(d.f.)[a]	7,730.56*** (66)	6,081.38*** (72)	7,224.27*** (67)	4,715.92*** (66)	6,341.27*** (62)
Rho (standard error)	-0.20 (0.03)	-0.31 (0.04)	-0.30 (0.05)	-0.24 (0.03)	-0.20 (0.03)
Wald test chi²(1)[b]	51.01***	62.48***	28.25***	76.85***	43.16***
Effect in standard deviations	-0.54	-0.18	-0.06	-0.06	0.05
Title I differential	-31.45	-19.64	-19.64	-14.64	-9.24
No treatment differential	-11.17	-14.38	-17.68	-12.58	-10.74
% change in achievement gap	185.32	37.40	11.50	16.88	-14.75

Minority Students

Linear Equation Estimates	1993–94 Reading		1995–96 Math		1997–98 Reading	
	4th grade		4th grade	8th grade	4th grade	8th grade
Title I Estimate (t-value)[a]	−6.13	(1.14)	1.19	(0.42)	8.82**	(2.49)	−4.50	(0.88)	4.12	(1.55)
N	27,018		30,609		23,288		30,171		24,304	
Wald test chi²(d.f.)[a]	3,275.93***	(68)	3,431.77***	(74)	3,203.70***	(71)	2,866.15***	(68)	3,052.64***	(64)
Rho (standard error)	−0.29	(0.09)	−0.34	(−0.06)	−0.36	(0.07)	−0.05	(0.10)	−0.20	(0.06)
Wald test chi²(1)[b]	9.22***		24.37***		23.40***		0.22		10.59***	
Effect in standard deviations	−0.16		0.04		0.26		−0.13		0.13	
Title I differential	−22.27		−13.20		−9.91		−7.01		−5.66	
No treatment differential	−16.14		−14.40		−18.73		−2.52		−9.78	
% change in achievement gap	38.50		−8.38		−48.80		−181.19		−43.93	

*10% significance level. **5% significance level. ***1% significance level.   (*t*-tests are two-tailed tests.)

NOTE: Exogenous coefficients are not reported.

a. Test for overall significance of achievement equations.

b. Test for independence of achievement and Title I equations.

Table 4-10 Effects of Title I on Achievement with Nonlinear Estimates for White and Minority Subsamples with Limited Variable List and State Fixed Effects

White Students Linear Equation Estimates[a]	1993–94 Reading 4th grade		1995–96 Math 4th grade		8th grade		1997–98 Reading 4th grade		8th grade	
Title I estimate (t-value)	-0.14	(0.10)	0.21	(0.13)	1.27	(0.44)	3.80**	(2.36)	5.47	(2.61)
N	64,155		66,172		58,556		62,674		55,752	
Box-Cox parameter	1.85		1.43		1.29		1.96		2.29	
Wald test chi²(d.f.)[b]	7,626.39***	(66)	6,012.06***	(72)	7,296.52***	(67)	5,180.18***	(66)	8,764.68***	(69)
Rho (standard error)	-0.56	(0.02)	-0.44	(0.04)	-0.34	(0.06)	-0.36	(0.03)	-0.30	(0.05)
Wald test chi²(1)[c]	317.51***		112.83***		31.48***		116.69***		35.80***	
Effect in standard deviations	-0.004		0.01		0.04		0.11		0.18	
Title I differential	-33.44		-20.31		-20.61		-15.40		-11.00	
No treatment differential	-33.30		-20.52		-21.88		-19.20		-16.46	
% change in achievement gap	0.44		-1.03		-6.00		-20.34		-35.00	

76

Minority Students
Linear Equation
Estimates[a]

| | 1993–94 Reading | | 1995–96 Math | | | | 1997–98 Reading | | | |
	4th grade		4th grade		8th grade		4th grade		8th grade	
Title I estimate (t-value)[b]	2.55	(0.59)	1.12	(0.39)	7.82**	(2.26)	-2.02	(0.37)	6.40**	(2.23)
N	27,018		30,609		23,288		30,171		24,304	
Box-Cox parameter	1.37		0.99		0.89		1.59		1.96	
Wald test chi²(d.f.)[b]	3,329.15***	(68)	3,433.38***	(74)	3,227.27***	(71)	3,101.72***	(68)	3,275.05***	(64)
Rho (standard error)	-0.45	(0.07)	-0.34	(0.06)	-0.34	(0.07)	-0.10	(0.11)	-0.26	(0.07)
Wald test chi²(1)[c]	34.33***		24.20***		21.73***		0.77		14.07***	
Effect in standard deviations	0.07		0.04		0.23		0.06		0.21	
Title I differential	-22.85		-13.20		-9.70		-7.06		-6.16	
No treatment differential	-25.40		-14.32		-17.52		-5.04		-12.57	
% change in achievement gap	10.14		-7.94		-46.25		-40.60		-53.02	

*10% significance level. **5% significance level. ***1% significance level. (t-tests are two-tailed tests.)

NOTE: Exogenous coefficients are not reported.

a. Estimates with Box-Cox transformations of achievement measures. Treatment effect estimates are scaled for conformity with untransformed achievement measures.

b. Test for overall significance of achievement equations.

c. Test for independence of achievement and Title I equations.

in the nonlinear equation from two of the minority subsamples, but two coefficients for white students are also positive and significant.

Tables 4-11 and 4-12 compare estimates for children ineligible for subsidized lunches with subsidized lunch students. As in earlier comparisons, Box-Cox transformations reduce to insignificance coefficients from linear equations that are large, negative, and statistically significant for some samples. For both tables comparing students classified by their income-conditioned eligibility for school lunch subsidies, only one positive and statistically significant coefficient emerges: the coefficient estimated for children from nonpoor families ineligible for subsidized lunches.

Minority students and those eligible for subsidized lunches overlap considerably.[19] Yet the estimated Title I effects are quite different for the two groups. In fact students eligible for subsidized lunches appear more similar to those who are not eligible than to minority students. Although there may be a hint in those results that Title I could be more effective for minorities than for white students, the evidence for such a difference is extremely weak in terms of the pattern of estimated coefficients and their statistical significance.

The tendency of the coefficients for minorities to be more positive than those for whites is the strongest evidence on the point that Title I could be more effective for minorities. In both tables 4-9 and 4-10 four of five estimates for minorities are larger than their counterparts for white students, although less than half the coefficients are positive and significant in both cases. In addition there are no large, negative, and statistically significant linear estimates for minority students for fourth grade in reading in 1993–1994 and for math in 1995–1996. That lack may indicate that the program may at least be less harmful for minorities than for other students in the earlier years. Except for the minority samples, however, the phenomenon of large, negative, significant coefficients for fourth graders in the earlier years is sensitive to functional form. And results for minorities should be relatively insensitive to functional form, given that their NAEP score distributions tend to be closest to normal among the student subgroups. In summary, estimated Title I effects for students from racial and ethnic minorities and children from poor families provide little support for a view that Title I has been particularly effective for them.

Interpretation

Summary of Results.   The preponderance of evidence indicates that Title I is not significantly improving student performance on state NAEP tests. Table 4-13 summarizes the size and significance of the treatment effect estimates in this chapter by grade, subject, subsample, model specification, and functional form. The table summarizes the size of estimated Title I effects by mean, minimum, and maximum effects in standard deviation units.

Of the eighty estimates reported in this chapter, the mean estimated Title I effect is less than one-tenth of a standard deviation, and the estimates range from −.60 to .27 standard deviations. To put the estimates in perspective, consider the black-white and subsidized lunch–nonsubsidized lunch gaps in NAEP scores. For the five samples examined, the gaps between black and white students range from −.88 to −1.11 standard deviations. Alternatively, when measured in percentage gaps relative to mean NAEP scores, the black-white gaps range from −10.80 to −16.33 percent. Less pronounced than the racial gaps, the gaps between nonsubsidized lunch and subsidized lunch students range from −.70 to −.86 standard deviations. Even the largest estimated Title I effect is not nearly adequate to close the achievement gap between less-advantaged and more-advantaged students.

Table 4-13 summarizes statistical significance in three categories: negative and significant, insignificant, and positive and significant. Summaries of statistical significance are presented at the customary .05 level of significance (in two-tailed tests). Of the eighty estimates of Title I effects reported in this chapter, eleven are negative, fifty-three are insignificant, and sixteen are positive.

Given that most estimates are small and insignificant, it is also important to consider whether there is any evidence that Title I has improved effects over time. The 1994 reauthorization of Title I shifted resources toward high-poverty schools and encouraged more schools to

Table 4-11 Effects of Title I on Achievement with Linear Estimates for Subsamples by Lunch Subsidy with Limited Variable List and State Fixed Effects

Nonsubsidized Lunch, Linear Equation Estimates	1993–94 Reading		1995–96 Math			1997–98 Reading	
	4th grade		4th grade		8th grade	4th grade		8th grade
Title I estimate (t-value)	-22.33***	(12.34)	6.88	(3.42)	3.21	(0.99)	-2.56	(1.39)	1.21	(0.69)
N	56,583		61,941		60,863		56,947		55,752	
Wald test chi2(d.f.)[a]	8,190.13***	(69)	6,183.50***	(74)	8,993.29***	(71)	3,372.20***	(68)	7,038.26***	(64)
Rho (standard error)	-0.15	(0.03)	-0.28	(0.04)	-0.22	(0.06)	-0.22	(0.03)	-0.19	(0.03)
Wald test chi2(1)[b]	26.82***		43.65***		12.00***		46.75***		33.81***	
Effect in standard deviations	-0.60		0.23		-0.09		-0.07		0.04	
Title I differential	-31.09		-20.38		-17.64		-14.64		-9.79	
No treatment differential	-8.75		-13.49		-14.43		-12.08		-10.99	
% change in achievement gap	260.69		-52.16		-23.34		-22.00		-11.60	

Subsidized Lunch Linear Equation Estimates

	1993–94 Reading 4th grade		1995–96 Math 4th grade		8th grade		1997–98 Reading 4th grade		8th grade	
Title I estimate (t-value)[a]	−9.90	(3.70)	−7.27	(1.67)	1.46	(0.36)	−3.72	(0.58)	2.85	(1.07)
N	38,383		38,356		26,045		39,617		26,990	
Wald test chi²(d.f.)[a]	5,532.87***	(69)	5,690.72***	(75)	5,484.84***	(72)	3,724.07***	(69)	3,859.35***	(65)
Rho (standard error)	−0.25	(0.05)	−0.15	(0.11)	−0.24	(0.07)	−0.10	(0.13)	−0.16	(0.06)
Wald test chi²(1)[b]	28.62***		1.94		7.83***		0.56		7.29***	
Effect in standard deviations	−0.26		−0.24		0.04		0.11		0.09	
Title I differential	−23.11		−13.25		−10.37		−8.57		−5.03	
No treatment differential	−13.21		−5.99		−11.83		−4.85		−7.88	
% change in achievement gap	75.73		122.48		−12.70		−77.13		−37.33	

*10% significance level. **5% significance level. ***1% significance level. (t-tests are two-tailed tests.)

NOTE: Exogenous coefficients are not reported.

a. Test for overall significance of achievement equations.

b. Test for independence of achievement and Title I equations.

Table 4-12 Effects of Title I on Achievement with Nonlinear Estimates for Subsamples by Lunch Subsidy with Limited Variable List and State Fixed Effects

Nonsubsidized Lunch, Linear Estimates[a]	1993–94 Reading 4th grade		1995–96 Math			1997–98 Reading	
	4th grade		4th grade	8th grade		4th grade	8th grade
Title I estimate (t-value)	−2.42*** (1.32)		−1.14 (0.57)	0.47 (0.13)		3.48* (1.81)	6.18*** (3.07)
N	56,583		61,941	60,863		56,947	55,752
Box-Cox parameter	1.82		1.45	1.31		2.02	2.16
Wald test chi^2(d.f.)[b]	8,445.00*** (69)		6,233.04*** (74)	9,175.10*** (71)		3,655.36*** (68)	7,390.43*** (64)
Rho (standard error)	−0.51 (0.03)		−0.41 (0.04)	−0.29 (0.07)		−0.34 (0.03)	−0.32 (0.03)
Wald test chi^2(1)[c]	179.12***		77.23***	14.47***		73.46***	46.30***
Effect in standard deviations	−0.06		−0.04	−0.01		−0.10	0.20
Title I differential	−33.16		−21.15	−18.93		−15.49	−11.63
No treatment differential	−30.73		−20.01	−19.41		−18.97	−17.81
% change in achievement gap	8.04		−5.81	−2.56%		−19.01	−36.58

82

Subsidized Lunch, Nonlinear Estimates[a]	1993–94 Reading	1995–96 Math		1997–98 Reading	
	4th grade	4th grade	8th grade	4th grade	8th grade
Title I estimate (t-value)[a]	−1.00 (3.70)	−6.80 (1.50)	1.12 (0.36)	−2.93 (0.49)	4.49 (1.49)
N	38,383	38,356	26,045	39,617	26.990
Box-Cox parameter	1.47	1.10	0.95	1.60	2.01
Wald test chi2(d.f.)[a]	5,693.32*** (69)	5,733.94*** (75)	5,483.06*** (72)	4,142.97*** (69)	4,253.76*** (65)
Rho (standard error)	−0.42 (0.04)	−0.15 (0.11)	−0.23 (0.10)	−0.12 (0.12)	−0.21 (0.07)
Wald test chi2(1)[b]	71.98***	2.11	7.75***	0.92	8.32***
Effect in standard deviations	−0.03	−0.23	0.03	0.08	0.14
Title I differential	−23.68	−13.30	−10.30	−8.65	−5.40
No treatment differential	−22.74	−6.50	−11.42	−5.72	−9.88
% change in achievement gap	4.20	105.40	−10.13	−51.54	−46.91

*10% significance level. **5% significance level. ***1% significance level. (t-tests are two-tailed tests.)

NOTE: Exogenous coefficients are not reported.

a. Estimates with Box-Cox transformations of achievement measures. Treatment effect estimates are scaled for conformity with untransformed achievement measures.

b. Test for overall significance of achievement equations.

c. Test for independence of achievement and Title I equations.

Table 4-13 Summary of Treatment Effect Estimates

Samples	Treatment Effects in Standard Deviations		
	Mean	Minimum	Maximum
All estimates (80 total)	0.005	−0.60	0.27
4th-grade estimates (48 total)	−0.07	−0.60	0.26
8th-grade estimates (32 total)	0.11	−0.09	0.27
Math estimates (32 total)	0.02	−0.24	0.26
Reading estimates (48 total)	−0.002	−0.60	0.27
Full sample estimates (40 total)	0.04	−0.38	0.27
White estimates (10 total)	−0.05	−0.54	0.18
Minority estimates (10 total)	0.06	−0.16	0.26
Nonsubsidized lunches estimates (10 total)	−0.07	−0.60	0.20
Subsidized lunch estimates (10 total)	−0.07	−0.26	0.14
Full model estimates (20 total)	−0.003	−0.60	0.27
Limited model estimates (60 total)[a]	0.03	−0.38	0.26
Regional dummies(20 total)	0.09	−0.32	0.27
State dummies (60 total)	−0.02	−0.60	0.26
Linear estimates (40 total)	−0.07	−0.60	0.26
Box-Cox estimates (40 total)	0.08	−0.23	0.27

Samples	Significance of Treatment Effect			
	Samples based on .05 level of significance			
	Negative	Insignificant	Positive %	Positive
All estimates (80 total)	11	53	16	20.00
4th-grade estimates (48 total)	11	33	4	8.33
8th-grade estimates (32 total)	0	20	12	37.50
Math estimates (32 total)	4	24	4	12.50
Reading estimates (48 total)	7	29	12	25.00
Full sample estimates (40 total)	6	24	10	25.00
White estimates (10 total)	2	6	2	20.00
Minority estimates (10 total)	0	7	3	30.00
Nonsubsidized lunches estimates (10 total)	2	7	1	10.00
Subsidized lunch estimates (10 total)	1	9	0	0.00

Full model estimates (20 total)	3	13	4	20.00
Limited model estimates (60 total)[a]	8	40	12	20.00
Regional dummies (20 total)	2	11	7	35.00
State dummies (60 total)	9	42	9	15.00
Linear estimates (40 total)	11	26	3	7.50
Box-Cox estimates (40 total)	0	27	13	32.50

a. Limited model specifications exclude class size, teacher education, teacher experience, homework, and TV variables.

operate schoolwide programs. Data are available for fourth-grade reading scores for 1993–1994 and 1997–1998. The pattern of estimates for fourth-grade reading scores between 1993–1994 and 1997–1998 varies widely by sample. Estimates for the full sample, whites, and nonsubsidized lunch students might suggest that the program may have been more effective (at least in the sense of being less harmful) in 1997–1998 than in 1993–1994. There is, however, no evidence from reading test scores that Title I has become more effective for fourth-grade minority and subsidized-lunch students. None of the estimates for minority and subsidized-lunch students are positive and significant for fourth-grade reading in 1993–1994 or 1997–1998. And in three of four cases, the fourth-grade reading coefficients became less positive over time for poor and minority students.

One might also question whether Title I tends to be more effective for a particular grade. Per pupil Title I expenditures were larger for fourth graders than for eighth graders. Interventions may also be more effective for younger students. Guryan (2001), for instance, finds that increased resources in Massachusetts had a positive effect on fourth-grade achievement but no significant effect for eighth graders. Accordingly one might expect to see greater effects for fourth graders than for eighth graders. Our estimates of Title I effects tend to be smaller and less significant for fourth graders than for eighth graders, however. The average estimated fourth-grade effect is –.07 standard deviations compared with .11 standard deviations for eighth graders. And although 37.5 percent of the estimated eighth-grade Title I effects are positive and significant, only 12.5 percent of estimates for fourth graders are positive and significant.

Title I could be more effective for eighth graders than for fourth graders for several reasons. A greater percentage of fourth graders in the sample received Title I benefits. By 1997–1998 half of fourth-grade subsidized lunch students and more than half of fourth-grade minority students in the state NAEP sample received Title I services. In contrast, 35 percent of eighth-grade minority and subsidized lunch students in the sample received Title I services in 1997–1998. Thus eighth grade may have been targeted more toward students who might have benefited from the program. There is some evidence of that targeting. When the sample is limited to minorities or subsidized lunch students, the selection bias is not significant for fourth-grade subsidized lunch students in 1995–1996 and 1997–1998 or fourth-grade minority students in 1997–1998. Selection bias for eighth-grade students is significant in all equations.

Title I effects could vary across subjects for several reasons. Parental involvement could be greater for reading than for math, for instance. Differences in estimated Title I effects for math and reading are not large, however. The mean estimate for math is .02 standard deviations compared with –.002 standard deviations for reading. And only 12.5 percent of math estimates are positive and significant compared with 25 percent for reading. On the whole there is little evidence that Title I has been effective in raising state NAEP scores in either subject.

Recent studies by Krueger and Whitmore (2001) and Grissmer and colleagues (2000) indicate that disadvantaged students may benefit more from additional resources compared with other students. Our evidence on the question is mixed, however. Eight of ten estimates for black, Hispanic, and Native American students exceed corresponding estimates for white students. For minority students, the mean Title I effect is .06 standard deviations compared with –.05 standard deviations for whites. Most estimates for both whites and minorities are insignificant, however. At the 5 percent level of significance, 30 percent of estimates for minorities are positive and significant, compared with 20 percent of estimates for white students. In addition, estimates for subsidized lunch students are not systematically more positive or more significant than

estimates for non–subsidized lunch students. Indeed none of the estimated Title I effects for subsidized lunch students are positive and significant at the 5 percent level.

State funding is now the largest category of government expenditures on elementary and secondary education.[20] In addition to expenditures, states might also influence achievement through policies such as
curriculum or testing. Specifications with regional dummies arguably
could be inappropriate, given that education policy is not made at the
regional level. Title I may account for part of the variation in achievement across states, however. Thus we estimate models with both state
and regional fixed effects. Estimates controlling for state fixed effects
tended to be somewhat smaller than estimates with only regional fixed
effects. The mean Title I effect from state fixed effect specifications is −.02
standard deviations compared with .09 for specifications with regional
dummies. Most estimates controlling for either regional or state fixed
effects were insignificant, however. Thirty-five percent of regional fixed
effect estimates are positive and significant at the 5 percent level, compared with 15 percent of state fixed effect estimates. Equations for student subgroups were estimated only with state fixed effects. Therefore,
fewer equations were estimated with regional fixed effects (twenty total)
than with state fixed effects (sixty total).

No theoretical reason calls for choosing a particular functional form
for student test scores. Box-Cox tests clearly rejected most linear specifications in favor of power transformation. Summary statistics also indicate
Box-Cox transformations result in more normally distributed test scores.
Estimates with Box-Cox transformations tend to be larger and more significant than their linear counterparts. The mean estimated Title I effect from
linear specifications is −.07 standard deviations compared with .08 for
models with Box-Cox transformations of test scores. A third of estimates
with Box-Cox transformed achievement measures are positive and significant, compared with only 7.5 percent of linear estimates. In addition, the
large (in absolute value) and highly significant negative linear estimates for
fourth graders in 1993–1994 tend to become insignificant when the
achievement measure is transformed. Title I could have a pronounced
negative impact on test scores, particularly if students were pulled out of

regular classrooms. The model with power transformations, however, could more adequately control for selection bias.

Limitations. Although we estimated the impact of Title I on student NAEP scores, the channels of influence are not entirely clear. Five variables that might be affected by Title I expenditures were examined: class size, a teacher graduate degree dummy, teacher experience, a dummy for students completing an hour or more of homework per evening, and student hours of TV viewing. Estimates controlling for those variables may underestimate the total effect of Title I on NAEP scores. Estimates not controlling for class size, teacher experience and education, homework, and TV measures could also be biased, however, because Title I funds do not necessarily affect those variables. We estimated equations that alternately included and excluded those variables.

When class size, teacher education, teacher experience, homework, and TV variables were excluded from the achievement equation, Title I effect estimates were on average slightly more positive. The mean Title I effect estimate with the five variables included is −.003 standard deviations compared with .03 when excluded. Thus, estimates controlling for class size, teacher education and experience, homework, and TV viewing may be biased slightly downward. We did not attempt to disentangle the separate influences of those variables, however. Other potentially more important channels of influence were not controlled for, such as teacher aides, for instance, for which data were not available.

Though suggestive, the results are subject to data limitations. Past as well as present educational inputs undoubtedly influence test scores. Historical information on educational inputs is unfortunately lacking in the NAEP data. That aspect limits the usefulness of NAEP data for estimating achievement relationships. Students are selected into Title I based on achievement, at least within schools. Therefore, the lack of information on earlier academic achievement is a particular limitation for analyzing the effects of Title I. The treatment effects estimator employed, however, is designed to control for latent differences between Title I and non–Title I students.

Policy implications. Many possible reasons exist for the lack of significant positive estimated Title I effects in this study. Title I may have systematic positive effects, but as discussed above, the NAEP may be inadequate for uncovering such relationships. Another straightforward possible explanation is that additional resources do not have systematic positive effects on student achievement. Indeed studies directly measuring the influence of additional resources on student achievement have inconsistent findings (see Hanushek 1998 for a review). For instance, Hoxby (2000, 1239) rules out "even modest effects" of class size on achievement. However, Krueger and Whitmore (2001) find significant effects of reduced class size, particularly for disadvantaged students.

Resources in sufficient quantity might have systematic positive influences on achievement, but Title I funding may be insufficient to produce any noticeable effects. Although Title I accounted for only 2.4 percent of total government expenditures on education in 1996–1997, for some areas the share of revenue from Title I is much larger than the average. From 1991–1992 to 1997–1998, 16 percent of students were in districts with a Title I share of total revenue of at least 4 percent; 4.4 percent of students were in districts where Title I accounted for at least 6 percent of total revenue, and 0.7 percent of students were in districts with at least 8 percent of total revenue from Title I.

Because all students in a district do not receive Title I services, Title I funding as a percentage of total funding per Title I student could be considerably more than the Title I share of total district revenue. Not all district revenues are used in ways that might be expected to benefit low-achieving students. Funding for teacher salaries may be more important for student performance than general revenue. The Department of Education estimates that Title I increased personnel expenditures 12 percent per student in schoolwide programs and 25 percent per Title I student in targeted assistance schools in 1997–1998 (DOE, OUS 2000). In addition, Grissmer and colleagues (2000) estimate that per pupil expenditures of $500–750 could raise achievement levels of disadvantaged students by one-third of a standard deviation. That range of expenditures is similar to Title I funding per pupil—for 1997–1998, $495 in elementary schools (DOE, PES 2001a).

Even if Title I expenditures per pupil are sufficiently large to increase student achievement noticeably, reductions in funding from other sources might offset funds received under Title I. A large literature addresses the fiscal response to intergovernmental revenue. Most studies find at least partial adjustments of own-source revenue from intergovernmental grants (see Hines and Thaler 1995 for a review), and some studies find total adjustments (for example, Becker 1996). Finance data are not nationally available at the school level. Using district-level data, Feldstein (1978) estimates an increase in total revenue of 80 cents in response to an additional dollar of Title I funds. Using more recent data for the 1990s, Gordon (2001) estimates that increases in Title I funding initially increase "school district revenue and instructional spending about dollar for dollar." After three years, however, the effects are no longer significant because of "local government reactions countering the effects of Title I" (Gordon 2001, 36).

A dearth of lasting Title I effects on district spending could explain weak and inconsistent evidence on the relationship between Title I and student performance. "Indeed, the common finding that Title I students exhibit no relative improvement could be entirely due to their having experienced few additional resources" (Gordon 2001, 2). Even if Title I funds have no net effect on district revenue, however, Title I could lead to the allocation of a larger proportion of district funds to activities intended to benefit disadvantaged students than if the district received no Title I funds.

Conclusions

This chapter presents new evidence on the relationship between Title I and student achievement based on state NAEP data. The data are the most recent large national data with information on both student Title I status and achievement. We analyze the student-level data for 1993–1994 (fourth-grade reading scores), 1995–1996 (fourth- and eighth-grade math scores), and 1997–1998 (fourth- and eighth-grade reading scores). Estimates of the impact of Title I on student NAEP scores range from −.6 to .27 standard deviations. Of the eighty estimates reported, only sixteen are positive and significant at the .05 level. The mean estimated Title I effect is close to zero (.005 standard deviations). To uncover possible effects of Title I, we consider flexible functional forms and a variety of model specifications. If Title I is having systematic positive effects on achievement, those results are not apparent from our analysis of the state NAEP data.

Although one might expect the impact of Title I to vary across subjects, there is little difference in estimates for math and reading. Inclusion or exclusion of variables potentially influenced by Title I (such as class size and homework) likewise make little difference. When separate equations controlling for either regional or state fixed effects were estimated, the estimated effects of Title I were generally less positive when controlling for state fixed effects. The differences between regional and state fixed effects estimates were small, however, and most coefficients were insignificant in both cases.

Estimates of effects for eighth graders were generally more positive and significant than for fourth graders, although even for eighth graders fewer than half the estimates were positive and significant at the .05 level. More positive results for eighth graders may seem surprising to those who think that earlier interventions should be more effective.

Several recent studies such as Grissmer and colleagues (2000) have reported that disadvantaged students may benefit more from additional resources than other students. Grissmer and colleagues (2000), however, did not estimate separate achievement equations for disadvantaged students.[21] This study, however, has separate equations estimated for minorities and subsidized-lunch students, subpopulations of students that may have the most to gain from Title I. We find no convincing evidence that Title I disproportionately benefits disadvantaged students. Although coefficients for minorities tend to be larger than their corresponding estimates for whites, most estimates are insignificant for both groups. In addition, we find scant evidence that subsidized lunch students benefit more from Title I than nonsubsidized lunch students.

The reauthorization of Title I in 1994 attempted to target Title I funds toward the poorest schools and hold schools more accountable for improvements in achievement. The 1994 reauthorization also made it easier for the poorest schools to operate schoolwide Title I programs. NAEP fourth-grade reading data are available before and after the reauthorization. Between 1993–1994 and 1997–1998, the pattern of results for fourth-grade reading students varies by sample. Estimates for the full sample, whites, and nonsubsidized lunch students tend to indicate that the program may have been more effective (at least in the sense of being less harmful) in 1997–1998 than in 1993–1994. Title I is not estimated to be more effective over time for minority and subsidized lunch students who took the fourth-grade reading test, however. In fact, coefficients for fourth-grade minority and subsidized lunch reading students tend to be smaller in 1997–1998. Moreover, none of the estimated coefficients for minority and subsidized lunch students in fourth-grade reading classes are positive and significant.

5

Summary and Conclusions

This evaluation of Title I discusses the goals of the program, describes the rationale for policies that have been pursued, and traces changes in the strategies intended to achieve program goals. Historical trends in achievement gaps—between black and white students and between schools with different incidence of poverty—illustrate the problem that the program addresses and indicate how far performance falls short of its goal. Analyses of the effects of participation in Title I have not shown consistent, significant effects on achievement. In view of changes in the rationale and implementation of the program over the years, the analyses raise questions about whether any approach that relies primarily on augmenting the flow of resources to poor schools is likely to be effective. The new Title I legislation, the No Child Left Behind Act of 2001, represents another in the continuing series of efforts to reform and improve its performance. Timely implementation of the new requirements for tests, publication of performance information, and sanctions for poor performance will help to provide early evidence on whether the more transparent approach lives up to its promise—or whether more-intensive reform, including a greater role for parental choice, may be needed.

The Program and Its Goals

When legislation establishing Title I was passed in 1965, hopes were high for its contribution to improving the performance of educationally disadvantaged children. The relatively poor performance of students in schools with high concentrations of children from low-income families was regarded in large part as a consequence of inadequate resources.

Providing increased funding for such low-income schools was considered key to bringing performance up to the level achieved in schools with average or high-income families.

Two main issues emerged in connection with the administration of Title I when the program began: (1) the extent to which funds went to the schools for which the program was intended and (2) whether money was being spent in ways that might be expected to help children directly. Some reports that funds were spent on amenities not obviously central to improving children's achievement came to public attention initially. To address those concerns, regulations and procedures were developed to specify what kinds of activities could be considered appropriate. The formulas for distributing Title I funds attracted considerable political attention, but developing criteria for the distribution of funds and determining whether funds were being distributed in compliance with the rules became fairly straightforward administrative functions. The regulations for the distribution of funds and accounting for their use were modified from time to time when the program was reauthorized. Over the years it became increasingly well documented that disproportionate shares of funds were allocated to schools with concentrations of children from low-income families. After the first few years, it became evident that if inadequate funding were the main source of the problem, the program should help to reduce disparities in achievement.

The need for studies to evaluate Title I to discover or confirm its effects on achievement was emphasized from the beginning of the program. Most early studies examining those effects failed to produce any convincing evidence that participation improved children's achievement. Despite the absence of favorable evidence on the effects of participation in Title I, the gap in test scores between black and white children gradually declined during the 1970s and the early 1980s. After the mid-1980s, however, test score gaps between children of different races and income levels showed no further narrowing. Moreover the results of more careful and detailed research that became available provided little evidence that the program was improving achievement.

Because the pattern of trends in test score gaps does not seem to correspond in any straightforward way to trends in Title I funding or policies, what factors might account for their initial narrowing and sub-sequent stability? In an analysis of the black-white test score gap, Hanushek (2001a) focused on desegregation, school funding, and changes in characteristics of families; he examined the pattern and esti-mated size of effects for "rough consistency with the measured student performance over time" (ibid., 27). He concluded that (1) changes in the level and distribution of funding could not account for changes in the gap; (2) increased school integration from the late 1960s through the 1970s could be responsible for most change; and (3) declining differ-ences between black and white students in parental education and fam-ily size might account for a small component of the reduction in the gap before it leveled off in the 1980s (ibid., 24–28).[1] The conclusions from that analysis are consistent with evaluations of Title I that show virtual-ly no significant effects of the program on achievement.

The accumulation of research evidence on the effects of Title I and experience with trends in achievement levels of elementary school chil-dren raised questions about the efficacy of programs and practices that had been developed for the remedial program. The shift in policy emphasis that resulted was in part a retreat from singling out Title I stu-dents for treatment and providing them with specific services (under pullout programs, for example) paid for by Title I. Attention shifted to raising standards and achievement for all students in schools with high proportions of children from poor families who received disproportion-ate shares of Title I funds. Instead of efforts to improve the performance of individual children identified as needing special services because of deficient achievement, raising the performance of all students in schools with high concentrations of children from low-income families was set as a goal.

A major transition in the implementation of Title I and the uses of Title I funds took place after the 1994 reauthorization legislation, which encouraged more widespread use of schoolwide programs. Our analysis of the effects of Title I examines experience before and after that transi-tion by using achievement data from NAEP tests for individual students during school years 1993–1994, 1995–1996, and 1997–1998. Consis-tent with most earlier studies, our analysis indicates that no systematic, significant positive effects on achievement can be traced to participation in Title I. Moreover there is no consistent evidence of more favorable effects of participation in Title I programs toward the end of the period covered by our data. Although evidence for some samples suggests the possibility that program performance may have improved, there is no indication that the effect of Title I on test scores for the most disadvantaged students has improved since the 1994 reauthorization. The weight of the evidence in our study points to (1) little or no positive effect of Title I on achievement and (2) no convincing indication of improvement over time.

Policy Implications

What can we conclude from our analysis and the results of many other studies of Title I over the past three decades? How should the lack of systematic effects on achievement from additional resources available to schools and students be interpreted? What are the implications for policy?

Perhaps the most basic point about Title I is that the problem addressed is real and important: reduction of systematic differences in achievement between different racial and ethnic groups or between income levels of families is a worthwhile goal, in part because of potentially beneficial effects on social and economic mobility. Because of the value of education and skills in the modern economy, smaller disparities in children's achievement could help to reduce the likelihood that low-income status perpetuates itself from one generation to the next. A program that succeeded in improving the performance of children with low achievement levels—especially when lower than average achievement is systematically associated with race or income—would make a valuable contribution.

After more than thirty-five years of experience and numerous careful efforts to evaluate its performance, the evidence has failed to demonstrate that Title I programs have been systematically and significantly contributing to reducing disparities in achievement by improving the performance of its beneficiaries. The different approaches taken over the years to administering the Title I programs have not led to the development of remedial programs that have reliably improved achievement. Experiments by federal, state, and local authorities and major shifts in the emphasis of federal policy have all failed to bring systematic improvement.

How can those conclusions be reconciled with the intuitively appealing idea that devoting more federal resources to schools in relatively low-income districts should help bring up achievement toward the level that prevails in higher-income schools? It is possible that much infusion of federal Title I money is offset by less money from local sources despite legislation and regulations intended to prevent such substitution. In that case potential effects of Title I could be dissipated by increased consumption by local taxpayers or more local government spending on other public services. Alternatively, if receipt of Title I funds actually does translate into higher total spending for schools, achievement may be unaffected because of the absence of any reliable relationship between resources and performance in the public school system.

The influence of family characteristics on children's achievement may be so important that their influence on achievement is difficult to offset with any remedial programs. The most authoritative and influential research on factors influencing children's achievement points to the overriding importance of long-term family characteristics. Some relevant characteristics, such as a family's emphasis on education, may be indexed in part by measures such as parents' education, but other characteristics that involve attitudes, habits of life, and culture are much more difficult to identify or measure. Although it may be extremly difficult to influence such family characteristics, policies that carve out a bigger role for families, that create incentives for parents to be better informed about their children's progress, and that afford families more choice about their children's education might have greater potential for improving achievement than resources, policies, and approaches developed and carried out by government with little role or responsibility given to parents.

This evaluation of Title I presents new evidence, consistent with most previous studies, that the federal program is not effectively contributing to its goal of reducing the achievement gap for educationally disadvantaged children. The policy implication of that study that seems most obvious is that the program should be phased out and shut down.

But the apparent failure of Title I to improve achievement of its participants does not imply that the schools receiving Title I funds and their
communities do not benefit from the program. The benefits involve
some combination of less revenue that needs to be raised from local
sources (along with the possible resulting increased consumption), more
funds from local sources available to finance other public services, and
federal funds to support professionals and aides employed by local
school systems. The political obstacles to phasing out and terminating
Title I are accordingly formidable because the program produces significant local public benefits under the rationale of improving education for
the disadvantaged—a goal that appropriately generates strong public
support. However welcome to its beneficiaries, continuation of Title I
under the argument that it serves as a resource flow to foster less inequality in resources among communities does not seem appropriate in the
absence of explicit modification by Congress of the goals of the program.

Any effort to eliminate or cut back significantly on funding for Title
I could be portrayed as abandoning the worthwhile goal of improving
the educational performance of disadvantaged children. Moreover, the
increase in funds authorized in the No Child Left Behind Act illustrates
the strength of contemporary pressures on Congress and the president to
support policies perceived by the public as demonstrating their commit-
ment to improving children's education. The trend toward devoting
more federal resources to compensatory education programs is not likely to be reversed in the absence of either greater public recognition of the
poor performance of traditional Title I policies or greater appreciation of
the potential for better performance of new approaches. Indeed, the por-
trayal of the new legislation by political spokespersons and the media as
a significant new approach was perhaps one important reason why the
increase in funding in the reauthorization attracted so much political
support. The new legislation does in fact introduce several changes that
could influence the performance of Title I. The potential of those
changes for improving achievement should be considered in light of
more than thirty-five years of experience with different program
approaches and evaluations of their effects.

Considering two conceptually different types of policies is helpful to structure a discussion of the potential for better Title I performance under the No Child Left Behind Act. The main differences between the two different types of policies involve the ways in which pressures to improve program performance are generated and how such pressures are translated into management decisions to make changes in programs to improve their performance. One type of policy envisages planning government programs, establishing goals, setting time schedules, monitoring performance, specifying remedies, and assessing penalties, with the federal government playing the lead role. In policies of that type, such government is seen as managing programs and taking the initiative in making changes. Historically Title I exemplifies that approach.

Another conceptually different type of policy approach could be described as a testing and information strategy. Under that type of policy, the government would develop procedures for systematic testing to measure students' achievement, encourage publication of test results, spell out performance criteria, and provide incentives for policy changes to address unsatisfactory performance. The goal of a testing and information strategy would be not only to facilitate improved government management of programs but also to enhance parental and community awareness of school performance. The strategy would make use of parents' decisions about supplemental services for their children and about schools where their children would be enrolled. The new legislation includes some initiatives that involve the second type of conceptual approach, in addition to provisions following the traditional approach to administration of Title I.

Some federal requirements for schools with poor performance records illustrate how some provisions of the recent reauthorization legislation follow the traditional approach to Title I. Funds can be spent only on activities validated by "scientifically based research." Low-performing schools must make "adequate yearly progress." States must establish starting points and timelines subject to federal guidelines for bringing students up to proficient levels in state assessments. The timelines for progress must be specified for racial, ethnic, and low-income categories, as well as for students with limited English proficiency or disabilities. The proficiency goals must be met within twelve years in annual steps (possibly including an averaging of test results over three-year periods). States must work with the federal government to establish suitable time paths for achievement by school and by student category and to deal with failure to achieve goals. Such failure to achieve "adequate yearly progress" goals will give rise to remedies that can include restructuring the school. In appropriate circumstances transferring students from a "failing" school to another in the district would be permitted, with the requirement that Title I funds would pay additional transportation costs. In some instances schools would need to use Title I funds to pay for supplemental services provided by state-approved vendors. Those new requirements in the legislation emphasize government design and management of Title I policies. Because those policies are conceptually similar to approaches pursued since the mid-1960s, they would seem to hold little promise for significantly better performance.

The effectiveness of the new Title I legislation may depend in part on the timeliness of implementing new requirements. The absence of evidence of improvement in Title I performance after the 1994 amendments has sometimes been attributed to their gradual and partial implementation. Some indications suggest that the federal government is giving a high priority to implementing the No Child Left Behind Act.[2] However, the long lead time for achieving goals (twelve years), the potential conflict between the pace for achieving goals and the adequacy of yearly progress, the small and uncertainly measured annual improvements required, and the modest remedies available to parents and communities when performance falls short suggest that prospects for major improvement in Title I performance are not favorable.

The recent reauthorization also includes new elements of a testing and information strategy providing for systematic year-by-year measurement of achievement gains and making information available about the achievement of children in different racial and income categories. Such information puts parents in a better position at least to monitor school performance and its impact on their children's peers. Although the reactions of parents to such information remain limited under the new legislation, the availability of systematic performance information at the local level is an initial step in improving awareness of parents and community leaders of needs for improvement and reform. Some preliminary evidence from experience in Chicago suggests that the testing and information strategy introduced there has improved student achievement; experience in Texas with "high-stakes" testing has also been favorable (Jacob 2002).[3] Those new testing and information requirements in the No Child Left Behind Act provide the main reasons for optimism about improving the contribution of Title I.

Enlarging the scope of parental choice about their children's schooling further enhances prospects for improving the contribution to achievement of Title I funds. The new legislation effectively limits parental choices to schools in the same district if their children's school has been determined to fall short of adequate yearly progress. In some instances, however, other schools in the district may offer little improvement. Opportunities for parents to respond to the performance of their local public school could also be extended to private schools. The Supreme Court decision in the Cleveland case (Zelman v. Simmons-Harris, 2002) removes questions about constitutional impediments to school choice that includes private religious schools. The tendency for parochial schools to be the main alternative to public schools in Cleveland is in large part attributable to the fact that voucher payments have been much smaller than the cost to government of paying for a child's education in public school systems. A broader range of private school alternatives emerged in Milwaukee, where voucher payments have been larger.

Because of the limited experience with school choice programs sufficiently generous to cover the full cost of schooling and uncertainties about many of their effects, a strong case can be made for taking an explicitly experimental approach: using some Title I funds to support adequately funded arrangements for school choice. Possible arrangements for experimental programs include simply devoting a substantial portion of Title I funds to vouchers to pay for public or private alternative schools. To provide sufficient funding to cover the full costs of alternative schools, at least partial matching of some kind from state and local sources could be required for participation in an experimental program. To allow enough time for significant adjustments in school resources to take place, the experiments should provide assurance of funding for at least a five-year period. Because of evidence that traditional Title I programs have not improved achievement, systematic experimental programs to extend a testing and information strategy with broader parental choice would be a promising investment in developing approaches that might be more effective.

Appendix

Table A-1 Achievement Equation Estimates

| | 1993–94 Reading | 1995–96 Math | | 1997–98 Reading | |
	4th grade	4th grade	8th grade	4th grade	8th grade
Title I student	-14.23*** (9.14)	-3.79** (2.29)	2.70 (1.20)	-2.77* (1.68)	1.63 (1.25)
Student age	-5.60*** (16.87)	-2.44*** (8.70)	-8.71*** (30.60)	-2.47*** (5.97)	-5.66*** (17.88)
IEP student	-32.59*** (36.85)	-24.03*** (28.87)	-29.71*** (27.82)	-32.95*** (23.11)	-29.28*** (28.31)
LEP student	-24.20*** (14.31)	-11.79*** (6.73)	-20.90*** (10.36)	-19.91*** (8.40)	-21.98*** (13.31)
Black	-16.28*** (26.48)	-16.50*** (31.49)	-20.99*** (34.24)	-12.60*** (16.89)	-15.66*** (28.59)
Hispanic	-14.39*** (23.29)	-11.34*** (22.10)	-12.98*** (19.88)	-11.75*** (16.19)	-10.08*** (17.78)
Native American	-6.31*** (6.34)	-8.70*** (11.14)	-11.03*** (8.02)	-8.79*** (9.06)	-7.58*** (5.98)
Asian	5.79*** (3.85)	3.00*** (2.73)	4.95*** (4.73)	4.66*** (3.22)	-4.38E-01 (0.51)
Female	6.08*** (19.51)	-2.70*** (11.99)	-4.36*** (15.02)	5.62*** (15.43)	8.28*** (27.78)
Subsidized lunch	-5.66*** (16.31)				
Free lunch		-3.88*** (24.39)	-5.52*** (11.85)	-12.05*** (23.89)	-6.39*** (14.49)
Reduced price lunch		-9.83*** (7.49)	-1.30** (1.96)	-6.10*** (8.65)	-1.98*** (3.06)
Hour or more of homework	3.71E-01 (1.09)	3.75E-01 (1.33)	4.36*** (13.72)	4.52E-01 (1.36)	5.75*** (19.48)
TV per day	-1.44*** (14.44)	-6.09E-01*** (8.12)	-1.95*** (19.16)	-1.67*** (13.92)	-1.60*** (15.55)
Reading materials	2.97*** (23.27)	2.76*** (25.49)	2.47*** (17.21)	3.08*** (17.90)	3.22*** (21.36)
Dad HS graduate	1.86*** (4.89)	1.18*** (3.59)	2.61*** (6.96)	2.44*** (4.88)	3.09*** (8.17)
Dad college graduate	3.86*** (10.17)	3.14*** (9.60)	8.00*** (16.47)	5.68E-01 (1.16)	7.30*** (16.55)
Mom HS graduate	4.74*** (12.21)	2.34*** (7.52)	4.46*** (11.14)	4.28*** (7.89)	3.51*** (8.00)
Mom college graduate	5.85*** (14.50)	4.43*** (13.59)	9.04*** (18.67)	2.34*** (4.19)	6.65*** (13.77)
Dad works		-1.79*** (4.46)	2.99*** (6.99)		
Mom works		-2.54E-02 (0.09)	-7.01E-01** (2.45)		

104

	(1)	(2)	(3)	(4)	(5)
Single parent	−5.43*** (14.43)	−4.30*** (11.52)	−1.90*** (5.31)		
Class size	8.78E-02** (2.44)	2.38E-02 (0.67)	1.67E-01*** (5.22)	1.07E-01*** (2.60)	3.14E-01*** (8.11)
Years teaching	1.28E-01*** (4.10)	9.13E-02*** (4.00)	1.31E-01*** (4.12)	1.29E-01*** (3.77)	5.29E-02* (1.93)
Graduate degree	−3.90E-01 (0.84)	8.06E-01** (2.21)	9.06E-01* (1.84)	4.83E-01 (1.00)	2.49E-01 (0.61)
School % black	−7.05E-02*** (3.99)	−9.70E-02*** (5.74)	−1.26E-01*** (6.62)	−1.09E-01*** (5.53)	−5.85E-02*** (3.53)
School % Hispanic	2.65E-02 (0.96)	−7.07E-03 (0.26)	−6.13E-02** (2.38)	−7.83E-03 (0.28)	4.14E-02** (2.08)
School % lunch	−1.50E-01*** (9.68)	−7.22E-02*** (6.00)	−5.25E-02*** (4.60)	−1.53E-01*** (8.37)	−1.16E-01*** (7.92)
Large city	4.50E-01 (0.32)	2.08 (1.55)	−1.59 (1.42)	1.67 (1.50)	−1.23 (1.28)
Midsize city	1.29 (1.45)	2.24* (1.93)	7.80E-01 (0.89)	2.41*** (2.60)	−2.00*** (2.75)
Suburb, large city	1.14 (1.10)	2.56E-01 (0.24)	1.04 (1.12)	1.06 (1.06)	−2.02*** (2.68)
Suburb, mid city	−3.08E-01 (0.33)	3.92E-01 (0.42)	−1.06 (1.33)	5.23E-01 (0.61)	−1.15 (1.62)
Large town	−.20** (2.23)	3.19*** (2.75)	2.48* (1.74)	2.17* (2.07)	1.40 (1.17)
Small town	1.75** (2.37)	8.90E-01 (1.18)	6.54E-01 (1.02)	3.00*** (4.37)	−1.03* (1.70)
District child coverty	−8.06E-02 (1.64)	−7.46E-02 (1.28)	−1.26E-01** (2.53)	−6.56E-02 (1.40)	−6.26E-02 (1.49)
Median Income	1.28E-05 (0.20)	1.82E-04*** (3.51)	2.00E-04*** (3.44)	5.21E-05 (0.80)	1.18E-04*** (2.46)
County, population 1–19%	−11.08 (0.54)	46.23** (2.36)	46.91*** (2.75)	−10.98 (0.47)	21.18 (1.27)
County, population 20–34%	−1.94 (0.12)	44.21*** (3.29)	69.26*** (5.34)	34.89** (2.13)	46.27*** (3.83)
County, population 60+%	1.46 (0.08)	58.19*** (3.86)	59.00*** (3.79)	24.54 (1.16)	44.62*** (2.85)
Constant	278.62*** (20.40)	211.77*** (17.86)	339.09*** (29.15)	236.49*** (16.09)	299.58*** (27.77)
N	94,966	100,297	86,908	96,564	82,742

* significant at .10 level   ** significant at the .05 level   *** significant at the .01 level. Numbers in parentheses are *t*-values.
Reported significance levels for *t*-tests are for two-tailed tests.
NOTE: Coefficients correspond to equations from table 4-5.   Equations also include state dummies (coefficients not reported).

105

Table A-2 Probit Estimates of Title 1

| | 1993–94 Reading | | 1995–96 Math | | | | 1997–98 Reading | | | |
| | 4th grade | | 4th grade | | 8th grade | | 4th grade | | 8th grade | |
	Coefficient	t-value	Coefficient	t-value	Coefficient	t-value	Coefficient	t-value	Coefficient	t-value
District Title 1 per pupil	4.71E-04	(3.26)	5.99E-04	(3.78)	2.67E-03	(13.38)	2.59E-04	(1.62)	2.03E-03	(8.73)
District child poverty rate	1.69E-02	(8.12)	1.01E-02	(4.87)	7.84E-03	(3.47)	8.24E-03	(3.45)	-6.29E-03	(2.27)
District % lunch program	1.56E-01	(1.19)	2.75E-01	(2.14)	-7.67E-02	(0.45)	3.15E-01	(2.11)	4.11E-01	(2.42)
District % black	-8.64E-01	(10.67)	-1.57	(18.66)	-1.36	(11.14)	-1.26	(14.43)	-1.60	(12.93)
District % Hispanic	-1.04	(8.49)	-8.90E-01	(7.36)	-1.70	(10.15)	-1.51	(10.81)	-1.00	(6.37)
School % lunch>=formula	9.76E-03	(15.83)	3.39E-03	(5.35)	1.38E-03	(1.41)	9.84E-03	(11.45)	1.09E-02	(9.43)
School % lunch<formula	6.76E-03	(3.05)	-1.53E-02	(7.83)	-6.39E-03	(2.54)	-1.20E-02	(4.37)	7.24E-03	(2.07)
Schoolwide threshold	1.38E-01	(4.21)	1.68E-01	(5.26)	2.84E-01	(6.58)	6.93E-01	(19.89)	5.70E-01	(13.34)
School % black	8.07E-03	(12.07)	1.82E-02	(27.82)	1.78E-02	(17.75)	1.20E-02	(17.31)	1.78E-02	(18.18)
School % Hispanic	9.90E-03	(10.27)	1.63E-02	(15.69)	2.18E-02	(15.55)	1.22E-02	(10.75)	1.60E-02	(11.85)
Large city	-3.09E-01	(8.49)	-1.08E-01	(2.80)	-8.82E-02	(1.61)	-3.31E-01	(8.87)	-5.78E-01	(12.85)
Midsize city	-2.91E-01	(10.26)	-1.29E-01	(4.71)	-3.79E-01	(8.95)	-2.91E-01	(10.26)	-4.45E-01	(12.34)
Suburb large city	-2.53E-01	(8.06)	-1.23E-01	(3.61)	-2.72E-01	(4.89)	-2.53E-01	(8.06)	-3.71E-01	(7.83)
Suburb midsize city	2.81E-02	(.76)	-2.54E-01	(8.38)	-2.81E-01	(6.19)	2.81E-02	(0.76)	-3.93E-01	(7.03)
Large town	-3.70E-01	(5.08)	-9.52E-02	(1.81)	-2.70E-01	(4.70)	-3.70E-01	(5.08)	-1.34E-01	(1.72)

	(1)	(2)	(3)	(4)	(5)
Small town	-7.06E-02 (2.93)	2.41E-02 (0.95)	-1.32E-01 (3.52)	-7.06E-02 (2.93)	-6.37E-02 (2.00)
Student age	8.05E-02 (4.08)	1.31E-01 (7.32)	1.11E-01 (5.00)	8.05E-02 (4.08)	5.99E-02 (2.71)
IEP student	-2.60E-02 (.49)	2.83E-02 (0.63)	8.14E-02 (1.16)	-2.60E-02 (.49)	-5.98E-02 (0.91)
LEP student	7.52E-02 (1.09)	3.71E-01 (5.86)	2.75E-01 (2.99)	7.52E-02 (1.09)	4.60E-01 (6.52)
Black	1.46E-01 (5.09)	1.98E-01 (7.64)	2.15E-01 (5.54)	1.46E-01 (5.09)	1.61E-01 (4.66)
Hispanic	1.18E-01 (3.78)	1.14E-01 (3.92)	1.45E-01 (3.61)	1.18E-01 (3.78)	7.63E-02 (1.76)
Native American	1.15E-01 (2.34)	1.76E-01 (3.68)	1.02E-01 (1.22)	1.15E-01 (2.34)	2.61E-01 (3.69)
Asian	-1.08E-01 (1.88)	2.29E-02 (0.41)	8.67E-02 (1.31)	-1.08E-01 (1.88)	5.30E-02 (0.80)
Female	-4.33E-02 (2.47)	-3.56E-02 (2.16)	-8.31E-02 (3.58)	-4.33E-02 (2.47)	-5.50E-02 (2.48)
Subsidized lunch	2.27E-01 (12.29)				
Reduced price lunch		1.91E-01 (6.27)	2.98E-01 (6.91)	2.54E-01 (8.22)	1.58E-01 (3.91)
Free lunch		3.74E-01 (18.22)	2.78E-01 (9.49)	2.36E-01 (10.80)	2.09E-01 (7.49)
Reading materials	-6.05E-02 (8.7)	-6.01E-02 (8.51)	-3.40E-02 (3.33)	-4.37E-02 (6.09)	
Dad HS graduate	-6.29E-02 (2.62)	-3.64E-02 (1.76)	-1.06E-01 (3.78)	-5.36E-02 (2.11)	-7.06E-02 (2.59)
Dad college graduate	-1.56E-01 (6.32)	-5.40E-02 (2.48)	-1.71E-01 (4.61)	-7.07E-02 (2.71)	-1.80E-01 (5.13)
Mom HS graduate	-8.21E-02 (3.38)	-5.04E-02 (2.47)	-8.78E-02 (2.93)	-5.30E-02 (1.95)	-2.30E-02 (0.80)
Mom college graduate	-6.82E-02 (2.74)	-1.14E-01 (5.11)	-1.68E-01 (4.35)	-6.33E-02 (2.27)	-4.69E-02 (1.31)
Dad works		4.94E-03 (0.20)	3.59E-02 (1.16)		
Mom works		-1.98E-02 (1.04)	-2.27E-02 (0.94)		
Single parent		7.55E-03 (0.34)	-2.02E-02 (0.77)		
Constant	-2.83 (7.64)	-2.66 (13.83)	-3.29 (9.93)	-2.03 (9.66)	-2.67 (8.29)
N	94,966	100,297	86,908	96,564	82,742
Wald test chi2(d.f.)	9,226.78 (71)	12,863.70 (77)	7,630.10 (74)	16,591.88 (71)	9,109.42 (67)
Pseudo R2	0.21	0.27	0.34	0.34	0.41

NOTE: Equations also include state dummies (coefficients not reported).

107

Notes

Chapter 1

1. Elementary and Secondary Education Act of 1965, Pub. L. 89-10, 79 Stat. 27 (1965).

2. *High-poverty schools* are defined as those with more than 75 percent of students eligible for subsidized lunches. *Low-poverty schools* are those with no more than 25 percent of students eligible.

3. There are three major NAEP assessments: the main NAEP, long-term trend NAEP, and the state NAEP. The main and state assessments occur in the winter after January 1. Long-term trend assessments are administered in fall, winter, and spring. DOE references all NAEP assessments by the new year (for instance, the 1994 NAEP assessments took place during the 1993–1994 school year). See DOE, NCES 1999 for detailed information on all NAEP assessments. Because figures 1-1 and 1-2 employ state NAEP data, sample averages may not be nationally representative: not all states were sampled. New Hampshire is excluded from figure 1-1: no high-poverty schools were sampled there.

4. Data in figures 1-3 and 1-4 were taken from DOE, PES 2001a and NCES 2002. Data for figures 1-3, 1-4, 1-7, and 1-8 are from the long-term trend NAEP, which provides the most appropriate data for comparisons over long periods.

5. Differences in average test scores for high-and low-poverty schools were computed as differences relative to average test scores for all students. Standard deviations for all students were used as the units for measuring differences for children from high- and low-poverty schools. Achievement gaps are commonly measured in standard deviation units (see Grissmer et al. 2000). Standard deviations of standardized test scores are fairly stable over time. Trends measured in percentage terms are consequently similar to trends measured in terms of standard deviations that are reported here.

6. Data in figures 1-5 and 1-6 are one author's calculations based on state NAEP data.

7. Gaps were computed as the difference between white and black scores relative to the mean for all students.

8. Similar trends in achievement gaps are present in data other than the NAEP data. For instance, Krueger and Whitmore (2001) found that the white-black gap in SAT scores narrowed from the 1970s through the early 1990s and widened starting in the mid-1990s. See also Jencks and Phillips 1998.

9. State white-black gaps, measured in standard deviation units, equal the difference between white and black scores relative to the state mean. The achievement gaps measured by NAEP scores can differ substantially from measures based in state tests. Klein et al. (2000) received much publicity for their RAND study comparing results of the Texas Assessment of Academic Skills (TASS) with Texas NAEP scores.

10. The 1994 reauthorization of Title I was part of the Improving America's School Act, which became law on October 20, 1994. The phase-in of most changes started during school year 1995–1996.

11. The 2002 reauthorization of Title I was part of the No Child Left Behind Act of 2001, Pub. L. 107-110, 115 Stat. 1425 (2002), which became law January 8, 2002.

12. Until school year 1997–1998, the federal government allocated Title I funds by county. Subsequently allocations went to school districts.

13. From DOE 2001a. The data reported here are adapted from exhibit 3, page 8.

Use of Title I Funds for Instruction, Instructional Support, and Program Administration, 1997–1998

Use of Funds	($ in millions)	Expenditures (percent)
Instruction		
teachers	3,342	47
teachers aides	1,043	15
all other forms	1,088	15
Instructional support	822	12
Program administration	35	12

Note: Percentages do not add to 100 percent because of rounding.
The category *instruction*—which includes teachers, teacher aides, and all other forms of instruction—sums to 77 percent for the 1997–1998 school year. The numbers are not materially different from a decade earlier. In 1987, 75 percent of Title I funds were reportedly used for basic instructional services (Congress 1987, 7).

14. Fifty percent of Title I funding goes to the highest-poverty districts, which contain only 25 percent of the nation's students; only 8 percent of Title I funds go to the lowest-poverty districts, also containing 25 percent of total students (DOE, PES 2001, 9). Further, distribution of Title I participation varies by grade

level, with elementary students representing a higher percentage, as shown in the following table, taken from DOE, PES 1999b, 12:

Participation in Title I by Grade Level
1996–1997

	(percent)	(in thousands)
Pre-K and K	12	1,320
Grades 1–3	37	4,070
Grades 4–6	30	3,330
Grades 7–9	15	1,650
Grades 10–12	5	550

15. DOE, PES 2001a, 80.
16. DOE, OUS 2000, 82–83.

Chapter 2

1. The first two chapters of McLaughlin 1975 discuss issues that arose when Title I was first implemented and how they were resolved.

2. By 1969 the multiplier for state per pupil expenditures was changed to the larger of the multiplier for the individual state or the national average (HEW 1969, 8).

3. Title I was enacted as part of President Lyndon Johnson's War on Poverty. A series of ambitious programs intended to break the cycle of poverty and promote a Great Society was enacted at that time. In addition to the Elementary and Secondary Education Act (Title I), programs included Medicare, Medicaid, Job Corps, Volunteers in Service to America (VISTA), Head Start (initiated by the Office of Economic Opportunity under the Economic Opportunity Act), the Higher Education Act, and a number of urban development, housing, and transit programs (Borman and D'Agostino 2001, 5–9).

4. The $2,000 income level, initially set only for the first year of the program, was raised to $3,000 by the 1966 amendments (applicable for FY1968). First the 1967 amendments and later the 1970 amendments delayed its application. The 1974 amendments finally raised the income level. See Congress 1987, 11–14.

5. Riddle 1986, 10, cites a 1981 study indicating that only nineteen LEAs in six states had adopted schoolwide plans.

6. The amendments passed in 1981 renamed Title I as Chapter 1. The 1994 amendments restored its designation as Title I, and this study refers to the program as Title I (Riddle 1994, 1).

7. The poverty rate data that are typically used for such determinations for individual schools are usually not based on the same poverty income thresholds established by the Census Bureau and used in the national allocation formula for LEAs. Most often the only poverty data available for children from individual schools are based on the number of children eligible for free or reduced-price school lunches (under income thresholds of up to 185 percent of the census poverty level) or the number of children in families receiving AFDC payments (with income thresholds varying by state). Thus the school-level poverty rate may be based on income levels that are much higher than the poverty income thresholds set by the Census Bureau (see Riddle 1992, 44, n 68, and 1994, 28, n 31).

8. The No Child Left Behind Act of 2001, Pub. L. 107-110, 115 Stat. 1425 (2002), became law January 8, 2002.

9. An index based on numbers of children from poor families would be an alternative. But some poor children in schools with few poor children may receive little or no Title I funding; some poor children in schools that received Title I funds may not need Title I services; and other children who are not from poor families but whose achievement is deficient may participate in Title I. Enrollment in elementary schools alone was used to measure number of pupils because Title I participants account for only a very small proportion of students in high school.

10. One anomaly of the system for allocating funds is that low-poverty schools on average receive more Title I funds per low-income student (about $1,000) compared with the average school or with high-poverty schools (about $615). Higher average funding per low-income student in the lowest poverty schools does not, however, mean less funding per student in need of assistance to improve achievement. That is, although Title I funds are allocated to school districts primarily on the basis of prevalence of children from low-income families, the ratio of children with low academic achievement to children from low-income families may be higher in low-poverty schools than in high-poverty schools. As a consequence Title I funds in low-poverty schools may need to be apportioned to more children than would be suggested by the proportion of children of poor families who are in low-poverty schools.

Chapter 3

1. McLaughlin 1975, 4–12, provides a good discussion of differences in emphasis on how evaluations should be done and how the results would be used.

2. The Sustaining Effects Study led to a series of twenty reports developed by System Development Corporation, Santa Monica. The results of the study are most accessible in an article written by the project director, Launor F. Carter (Carter 1984, 4–13). The Prospects Study was carried out by Abt Associates Inc., Bethesda, Maryland. Puma et al. 1997 summarizes the results.

3. Reauthorization of Title I in the 1994 amendments to the ESEA mandated the more recent report carried out with the assistance of an independent review panel (DOE, PES 1999b).

4. The Sustaining Effects Study mandated by Congress began in 1975 (Carter 1984, 4).

5. Although the estimate from the Prospects Study may seem high in view of the small share of total spending on elementary and secondary education accounted for by Title I funds, Title I funds were allocated disproportionately to high-poverty schools; in those schools Title I services were targeted to children with low achievement.

6. Subsequent analysis confirmed the validity of this approach to defining a comparison group. For instance, see Borman and D'Agostino 1996, 315.

7. The gap in fourth-grade math scores between high- and low-poverty schools was twenty points in 1986, compared with twenty-one points in 1996 (DOE, NCES 1999, vi, exh. 3).

8. The meta-analysis is an ambitious effort to summarize research evaluating the effects of Title I on achievement. The authors began by identifying 150 studies; 81 were selected for more careful review, and 17 that met reasonable quantitative standards were summarized. A later version of the paper (Borman and D'Agostino 2001) argues that the impact of Title I has become more positive since the 1970s. A trend toward more positive effects is at odds, however, with the stagnation of gaps in NAEP test scores during the late 1980s and the 1990s.

9. Wayne Riddle has monitored and reported on legislative developments on Title I and other education initiatives for Congress and has reviewed and summarized research reports assessing performance of the program over the years. The summary statement follows his brief review of the findings of major studies of Title I.

Chapter 4

1. The source paper, in which additional technical detail is available on the analysis discussed in this chapter, is Mast 2002.

2. The High School and Beyond and National Education Longitudinal Survey data contain information on the school share of students receiving Title I but no student-level Title I information. The data sets are not well suited to evaluating Title I because only a small percentage of high school students receive Title I services.

3. In 1990 state NAEP assessments began testing fourth and eighth graders with the same exams and methodology employed in the main NAEP (DOE, NCES 1999). Exclusion of twelfth graders from the state NAEP is not a serious drawback for the study because only a small percentage of high school students receive Title I services.

4. The fourth-grade samples include forty-one states in 1993–1994, forty-three states and the District of Columbia in 1995–1996, and forty states and the

District of Columbia   in 1997–1998;   eighth-grade samples for those years include forty-one states, forty states and the District of Columbia, and thirty-six states and the District of Columbia. Models were also estimated without Alaska, Hawaii, and the District of Columbia. The estimates were similar to actual reported scores. For example, when the fourth-grade math model in table 1-7 with regional controls is estimated excluding Alaska, Hawaii, and the District of Columbia, the estimated treatment effects (t-statistics) are 3.51 and 1.27. The corresponding estimates (t-statistics) in table 4-7 are 3.81 and 1.41.

5. Estimates were also made by using each of the five plausible values as dependent variables. The estimates were similar to those using the mean of the five values as a dependent variable. For example, when the model in table 4-5 for fourth graders in 1993–1994 is estimated with the five plausible NAEP values, the estimated treatment effects (t-values) are –14.55 (8.74), –13.72 (7.92), –14.08 (8.43), –14.40 (8.61), and –13.71 (8.15). The estimated (t-value) reported in table 4-5 using the mean of the five plausible values as a dependent variable is –14.23 (9.14). The Department of Education suggests computing point estimates of coefficients based on averages of coefficients estimated with the five plausible values and describes a method for computing the standard errors using replicate techniques (NCES 2000b). This study did not use that method because of the sample selection model estimated. The large sample sizes also make replicate methods burdensome.

6. One cannot definitively determine which schools in the sample are operating schoolwide programs. The NAEP data have no information on schoolwide status. Although data are available on the percentage of students receiving Title I services, all students could qualify in the absence of schoolwide authority. Discrepancies also exist between student and school Title I information in the NAEP data. In any event, when a dummy variable was included in the achievement equations for schools with all students reportedly receiving Title I services, the coefficients estimated for the variable were positive.

7. Evidence from the main NAEP might be more conclusive on how characteristics of Title I students changed because that sample is nationally representative. This chapter later presents evidence on targeting based on Wald tests for selection bias (unmeasured differences between Title I and non–Title I students). Tests for fourth-grade poor and minority students indicate recent changes are focusing Title I resources less toward low-performing poor and minority students (see discussion on page 63).

8. IEP status might be systematically related to Title I status. The correlations between the Title I and IEP dummies are slight, however. The weighted correlations (p-values) for fourth-grade reading in 1993–1994; fourth-grade math, eighth-grade math, and fourth-grade reading in 1997–1998; and eighth-grade reading are respectively -.001 (.75), -.008 (.01), .005 (.14), -.002 (.58), and -.02 (.01). For fourth-grade math, for example, 30.5 percent of non-IEP students received Title I services, compared with 30.2 percent of IEP students.

9. Continuous measures of TV viewing, reading materials in the home, and years teaching were constructed from categorical data for all years. Midpoints were used for bounded categories, and minimum points were used for open-ended categories. For some years, class size and percent of students eligible for lunch programs were also constructed from categorical data.

10. Numerous studies have found a significant relationship between demographics and support for public education. For example, Hoyt and Toma 1993 found a positive relationship between median age and education spending. Poterba 1997, 1998, and Ladd and Murray 2001 found that the demand for public education funding was negatively related to the elderly share of the population.

11. State dummies do not control for important unmeasured effects within states. For instance, districts and schools have considerable discretion in the use of Title I funds. Models with district or school fixed-effects could help control for unmeasured factors within states. However, controlling for selection bias in such models is difficult. Because many districts and schools have no variation in the Title I student dummy, a probit cannot be estimated with district or school fixed-effects. Furthermore, as discussed below, instruments in the Title I equation used to identify the achievement equation are school or district-level variables. It is difficult to imagine a student characteristic that would affect Title I status but have no independent impact on achievement. Therefore, identification of the achievement equation would be based solely on nonlinearity of the Title I equation in models with school fixed-effects.

12. Student age was imputed for any student with reported age greater than two years from the mean. Missing values were imputed by a Markov-chain Monte Carlo process. Imputations were based on all nonmissing exogenous variables; student NAEP scores and Title I status were not employed in the imputation process. For each missing NAEP variable, five values were imputed. Missing values were replaced with the median of the five imputed values.

13. A common problem with cost indexes is their basis on prices determined by supply and demand. For example, Dumond, Hirsch, and MacPherson 1999 estimated that metropolitan cost-of-living indexes based on Chamber of Commerce price data overstated wage differentials based on the cost of living by 60 percent because of differences in demand. See Ginsburg, Noell, and Rosenthal 1985 for a more detailed discussion of state per pupil expenditures in the Title I formula.

14. Data on Title I student populations by district are not available during the sample period (they are determined by school and student participation). Title I equations were also estimated with Title I funds per student below the poverty line and per subsidized-lunch student in place of the district poverty rate and percentage of students receiving subsidized lunches. Title I per poor or subsidized-lunch student is undefined for some districts. In addition, the range of the variables is much greater than for Title I per student, possibly because of some

low-poverty districts receiving Title I funds or measurement error. For example, between 1991–1992 and 1997–1998, district Title I per student ranged from $0 to $8,048 (in real 1997 dollars) with a mean of $147. Title I per student below the poverty line (per subsidized-lunch student) ranged from $0 ($0) to $357,706 ($926,772) with a mean of $1000 ($699). Nonetheless, estimates with those variables in the Title I equation are similar to those reported. The source for school district finance was the Census Bureau's Elementary/Secondary School Finance Data. District demographic data were extracted from the Department of Education's Local Education Agency Universe Survey Data.

15. The difference in achievement between Title I and other students is estimated as treatment effect + (rho)σ(hazard), where rho is the correlation between the error terms of the probit and achievement equations, and σ is the coefficient of the hazard from the Title I probit equation. (Rho)σ(hazard) is the estimated achievement gap absent Title 1 services. See Greene 1993 and Maddala 1983 for more detailed information on the estimator for treatment effects.

16. For the merged sample the mean weight is approximately 27. Thus the average student in the sample had a 1/27 probability of being sampled and represents 27 students in the population.

17. The Department of Education suggests using jack-knife methods to account for the NAEP survey methodology (cluster sampling). Computing limitations prevented estimating jack-knife standard errors for all the variables controlled for in this study. Jack-knife standard errors were estimated for models with a limited set of exogenous variables. The jack-knife standard errors for those models were virtually identical to the standard errors computed with the common Taylor-expansion method employed for this study.

18. The Box-Cox transformation of the variable Y is $(Y^\theta-1)/\theta$, where θ is the Box-Cox parameter.

19. Sixty-six percent of blacks, Hispanics, and Native Americans in the merged sample receive subsidized lunches compared with 23 percent of white students. Of subsidized lunch students in the merged sample, 59 percent were black, Hispanic, or Native American and 37 percent were white.

20. In 1996–1997, state funding was 49.3 percent of total government expenditures on elementary and secondary education compared with 44.0 percent for local governments and 6.8 percent for the federal government (DOE, NCES, 2000a).

21. Grissmer et al. 2000 based its conclusion regarding disadvantaged students on an interaction between school resource and socioeconomic status variables. See Hanushek 2001b for a critical review of that methodology.

Chapter 5

1. Hanushek described the black-white gap in NAEP scores as approximately one standard deviation in the 1990s, a gap about .3 standard deviations

smaller than in the 1970s. The estimates Hanushek reported suggest that more integration could by itself account for a decline of .4 to .5 standard deviations. The predicted effects of changes that he considered as affecting the test score gap—more integration and smaller differences in parental education and family size—accounted for a larger reduction in the gap than its actual decline from the 1970s to the 1990s. Those estimates cast doubt on the idea that Title I contributed to narrowing the achievement gap in the 1970s and the early 1980s.

2. Some organized resistance to changes introduced by the No Child Left Behind Act has already emerged at the local level according to anecdotal evidence in newspaper reports. Efforts have apparently been made to discourage parents from transferring children from failing schools to schools that perform better. See, for example, Schulte 2002 and Levine 2002.

3. Jacob discussed similarities between the No Child Left Behind Act and the test-based accountability policy implemented in the Chicago public schools in 1996–1997. He found that math and reading achievement (as measured by the high-stakes examinations) increased sharply, by an estimated two- to three-tenths of a standard deviation, following the introduction of the policy in Chicago.

References

Becker, Elizabeth. 1996. "The Illusion of Fiscal Illusion: Unsticking the Flypaper Effect." *Public Choice* 86: 85–102.

Borman, Geoffrey D., and Jerome V. D'Agostino. 1996. "Title I and Student Achievement: A Meta-Analysis of Federal Evaluation Results." *Educational Evaluation and Policy Analysis* 18 (4) (winter): 309–26.

———. 2001. "Title I and Student Achievement: A Quantitative Synthesis." In *Title I: Compensatory Education at the Crossroads,* edited by Geoffrey A. Borman, Samuel C. Stringfield, and Robert E. Slavin, pp. 25–58. Mahwah, N.J.: Lawrence Erlbaum Associates.

Carter, Launor F. 1984. "The Sustaining Effects Study of Compensatory and Elementary Education." *Educational Researcher,* August–September, pp. 4–13.

Coleman, James S., et al. 1966. *Equality of Educational Opportunity.* Washington, D.C.: Government Printing Office (GPO).

Downes, Thomas A., and David N. Figlio. 1998. "School Finance Reforms, Tax Limits, and Student Performance: Do Reforms Level-Up or Dumb Down?" Working paper, Tufts University, Boston.

Dumond, J. Michael, Barry T. Hirsch, and David A. MacPherson. 1999. "Wage Differentials across Labor Markets and Workers: Does Cost of Living Matter?" *Economic Inquiry* 37 (4) (October): 577–98.

Eddinger, Lucille. 1969. "Private Study Charges Local Misuse of U.S. Funds for Impoverished Pupils." *National Journal* 1 (3) (November 15): 124–25.

Feldstein, Martin S. 1978. "The Impact of a Differential Add-on Grant: Title I and Local Education Spending." *Journal of Human Resources* 13 (4) (fall): 443–58.

Ginsburg, Alan L., Joy Noell, and Alvin S. Rosenthal. 1985. "Is the Federal Chapter 1 Formula Equitable?" *Journal of Education Finance,* 10 (3) (winter): 360–74.

Gordon, Nora. 2001. "Do Federal Grants Boost School Spending? Evidence From Title I." Working paper, Harvard University, Cambridge.

Greene, William H. 1993. *Econometric Analysis.* 2nd ed. New York: Macmillan.

Grissmer, David W., Anne Flannigan, Jennifer Kawata, and Stephanie Williamson. 2000. *Improving Student Achievement: What NAEP State Test Scores Tell Us.* Santa Monica, Calif.: RAND.

Guryan, Jonathan. 2001. "Does Money Matter?   Regression Discontinuity Estimates from Education Finance Reform In Massachusetts." NBER Working Paper 8269, National Bureau of Economic Research, Cambridge, Mass.

Hanushek, Eric A. 1998. "Conclusions and Controversies about the Effectiveness of School Resources." Federal Reserve Bank of New York *Economic Policy Review* 4 (March): 11–27.

————. 1999. "Budgets, Priorities, and Investment in Human Capital." In *Financing College Tuition, Government Policies and Educational Priorities,* edited by Marvin H. Kosters, pp. 8–27. Washington, D.C.: AEI Press.

————. 2001a. "Black-White Achievement Differences and Governmental Interventions." *American Economic Review* 91 (2): 24–28.

————. 2001b. "Deconstructing RAND." *Education Matters* 1 (1) (spring): 65–70.

Hines, James R. Jr, and Richard H. Thaler. 1995. "Anomolies: The Flypaper Effect." *Journal of Economic Perspectives* 9 (4) (fall): 217–26.

Hoxby, Caroline M. 2000. "The Effects of Class Size on Student Achievement: New Evidence from Population Variation." *Quarterly Journal of Economics* 115 (4) (November): 1239–85.

Hoyt, William H., and Eugenia F. Toma. 1993. "Lobbying Expenditures and Government Output: The NEA and Public Education." *Southern Economic Journal* 60 (2) (October): 408–17.

Jacob, Brian A. 2002. "Accountability, Incentives and Behavior: The Impact of High-Stakes Testing in the Chicago Public Schools." NBER Working Paper 8968, National Bureau of Economic Research, Cambridge.

Jencks, Christopher, and Meredith Phillips, eds. 1998. *The Black-White Test Score Gap.* Washington, D.C.: Brookings Institution Press.

Jennings, John F. 2000. "Title I, Its Legislative History and Its Promise." *Phi Delta Kappan* (March): 516–22.

Klein, Stephen P., Laura S. Hamilton, Daniel F. McCaffrey, and Brian M. Stecher. 2000. "What Do Test Scores in Texas Tell Us?" RAND issue paper, RAND, Santa Monica, Calif.

Krueger, Alan B., and Diane M. Whitmore. 2001. "Would Smaller Classes Help Close the Achievement Gap?" In *Bridging the Achievement Gap,* edited by John E. Chubb and Tom Loveless, pp. 11–46. Washington, D.C.: Brookings Institution.

Ladd, Helen F., and Sheila E. Murray. 2001.   "Intergenerational Conflict Reconsidered: County Demographic Structure and the Demand for Public Education." *Economics of Education Review* 20 (4) (August): 343–57.

Levine, Susan. 2002. "Few Families Seek School Switch in Montgomery." *Washington Post,* June 22.

Maddala, G. S. 1983. *Limited Dependent and Qualitative Variables in Econometrics.* Cambridge: Cambridge University Press.

Mast, Brent. 2002. "Title I and Academic Achievement: Evidence from the State NAEP." Working paper, American Enterprise Institute, Washington, D.C.

McLaughlin, Donald H. 1977. *Title I, 1965–1975: A Synthesis of the Findings of Federal Studies.* Report for the National Institute of Education, American Institutes for Research, Palo Alto, Calif.

McLaughlin, Milbrey W. 1975. *Education Evaluation and Reform: The Elementary and Secondary Act of 1965, Title I.* Cambridge, Mass.: Ballinger.

Mullin, Stephen P., and Anita A. Summers. 1983. "Is More Better? The Effectiveness of Spending on Compensatory Education." *Phi Delta Kappan,* pp. 339–47.

Murray, Sheila E., William N. Evans, and Robert M. Schwab. 1998. "Education-Finance Reform and the Distribution of Education Resources." *American Economic Review* 88 (4) (September): 788–812.

Poterba, James M. 1997. "Demographic Structure and the Political Economy of Public Education." *Journal of Policy Analysis and Management* 16: 45–66.

———. 1998. "Demographic Change, Intergenerational Linkages, and Public Education." *American Economic Review Papers and Proceedings* 88 (3) (May): 315–20.

Puma, Michael J., Nancy Karweit, Cristofer Price, Anne Ricciuti, William Thompson, and Michael Vaden-Kiernan. 1997. *Prospects: Final Report on Student Outcomes.* Cambridge, Mass.: Abt Associates.

Riddle, Wayne C. 1986. "Chapter 1, Education Consolidation and Improvement Act Grants to Local Educational Agencies for the Education of Disadvantaged Children: Selected Reauthorization Options and Alternatives." Washington, D.C.: Congressional Research Service

———. 1992. "Chapter 1 B Education for Disadvantaged Children: Background and Issues." CRS Report for Congress, 92-878 EPW. Washington, D.C.: Congressional Research Service.

———. 1994. "Education for the Disadvantaged: Analysis of 1994 ESEA Title I Amendments under P.L. 103-382." CRS Report for Congress, 94-068 EPW. Washington, D.C. Congressional Research Service.

———. 1996. "Title I, Education for the Disadvantaged: Perspectives on Studies of Its Achievement Effects." CRS Report for Congress, 96-82 EPW. Washington, D.C. Congressional Research Service.

Schulte, Brigid. 2002. "For Pupils, A Chance to Transfer Up." *Washington Post,* May 10.

U.S. Commission on Civil Rights. 1967. *Racial Isolation in the Public Schools.* Washington, D.C.: GPO.

U.S. Congress, Committee on Education and Labor, Subcommittee on Elementary, Secondary and Vocational Education. 1987. "Federal Assistance for Elementary and Secondary Education: Background Information on Selected Programs Likely to Be Considered for Reauthorization by the 100th Congress." Washington, D.C.: GPO.

U.S. Department of Education, National Center for Education Statistics. 1999. *The NAEP Guide,* NCES 2000-456, edited by N. Horkay. Washington, D.C.: GPO.

―――. 2000a. *Digest of Education Statistics.* NCES 2000-031, by Thomas D. Snyder and Charlene Hoffman. Washington, D.C.: GPO.

―――. 2000b. *The NAEP Data Toolkit: Tutorial and Reference Guide.* NCES review draft version 1.6.

U.S. Department of Education, Office of the Under Secretary, Planning and Evaluation Service. 1997. *Prospects: Final Report on Student Outcomes,* prepared by Michael J. Puma, Nancy Karweit, Cristofer Price, Anne Ricciuti, William Thompson, and Michael Vaden-Kiernan, Abt Associates. Washington: D.C.: GPO.

―――. 1999. *Promising Results, Continuing Challenges: The Final Report of the National Assessment of Title I.* Washington, D.C.: GPO.

―――. 2001a. *High Standards for All Students: A Report from the National Assessment of Title I on Progress and Challenges since the 1994 Reauthorization.* Washington, D.C.: GPO.

―――. 2001b. *The Longitudinal Evaluation of School Change and Performance (LESCP) in Title I Schools.* Final report: vol. 1, *Executive Summary,* and vol. 2, *Technical Report,* prepared by Westat and Policy Studies Associates. Washington, D.C.: GPO.

U.S. Department of Education, Office of the Under Secretary, Planning and Evaluation Service, Elementary and Secondary Education Division. 1996. *Mapping Out the National Assessment of Title I: The Interim Report.* Washington, D.C.: GPO.

―――. 2000. *Study of Education Resources and Federal Funding: Final Report.* Washington, D.C.: GPO.

―――. http://www.ed.gov/offices/OUS/PES/ed_for_disadvantaged.html#fact-sheet, accessed January 11, 2002.

U.S. Department of Health, Education, and Welfare, Office of Education. 1969. "History of Title I ESEA." Mimeo.

U.S. Government Accounting Office. 2000. *Title I Program Stronger Accountability Needed for Performance of Disadvantaged Students,* GAO/HEHS-00-89. Washington, D.C.: GPO.

Vinovskis, Maris A. 1999. "Do Federal Compensation Education Programs Really Work?" *American Journal of Education* (May), pp. 187–209.

Wargo, Michael J., G. Kasten Tallmadge, Debbra D. Michaels, Dewey Lipe, and Sarah J. Morris. 1972. *ESEA Title I: A Reanalysis and Synthesis of Evaluation Data from Fiscal Year 1965 through 1970.* Palo Alto: American Institutes for Research in the Behavioral Sciences.

Index

About the Authors

Marvin H. Kosters is a resident scholar at AEI. His research areas include the labor market, government regulation, and education. Mr. Kosters is the author or editor of several books, including *Workers and Their Wages: Changing Patterns in the United States* (1991), *Trade and Wages: Leveling Wages Down?* (1994), *The Effects of the Minimum Wage on Employment* (1996), *Wage Levels and Inequality: Measuring and Interpreting the Trends* (1998), and *Financing College Tuition: Government Policies and Educational Priorities* (1999). He received a Ph.D. in economics from the University of Chicago.

Brent D. Mast, a research fellow at the Progress and Freedom Foundation, has taught economics at Hobart and William Smith Colleges, John Jay College of Criminal Justice of the City University of New York, and Miami University of Ohio. His research focuses on education, public choice, and crime. He is the coauthor of *Income Redistribution from Social Security* (forthcoming). Mr. Mast received his Ph.D. in economics from Florida State University.